recover and rebuild

DOMESTIC VIOLENCE WORKBOOK

recover
and
rebuild

moving on
from
partner abuse

DOMESTIC VIOLENCE WORKBOOK

Stacie Freudenberg, PsyD

ROCKRIDGE PRESS

Interior and Cover Designer: John Clifford
Art Producer: Samantha Ulban
Editor: Barbara J. Isenberg
Production Editor: Andrew Yackira

Cover Art © Shutterstock/sergio43. All other images used under license © Creative Market/M. by mprintly.

ISBN: Print 978-1-64611-052-0 | eBook 978-1-64611-053-7

R0

CONTENTS

INTRODUCTION

This workbook is intended for adult survivors of relationship abuse, also referred to as domestic violence, emotional abuse, intimate partner violence, relational abuse, or domestic abuse. If you've experienced an abusive relationship and managed to leave, be proud of yourself! Leaving is the first step in starting a new life, free from abuse, and completing this book can help you on that journey. Unfortunately, for many survivors, there are a lot of hurdles to face after leaving. This book will help you on your journey to heal and move forward. If you're still in an abusive relationship, this book may not be helpful, as many of the exercises are designed specifically for someone who has already left the relationship. Attempting some of these exercises while still in an abusive relationship is not advised because they may increase emotionally and physically abusive behaviors by a perpetrator. Additionally, healing from trauma can be difficult while still experiencing trauma. Unfortunately, this book is not intended to assist someone with a safe exit. If you're experiencing an abusive relationship and would like support, please call the 24/7 National Domestic Violence Hotline at 1-800-799-7233. Advocates will be waiting to assist you and can help you locate services in your area.

Domestic violence affects every gender, ethnicity, and sexual orientation. There is a common misconception that abusive relationships are primarily experienced by heterosexual partners, with males being the perpetrators. This is widely untrue, and research has shown that LGBTQ+ individuals experience similar, and sometimes higher, rates of domestic violence compared to individuals in heterosexual relationships. Additionally, females can also be perpetrators. Most books are written specifically for women who have experienced domestic violence and assume that their abusers are male. To date, there are very few books that address domestic violence from a gender-inclusive perspective, which is the aim of this workbook. I hope this book will assist anyone who has experienced an abusive relationship, regardless of how they identify. This book takes a strengths-based approach and is intended to be inclusive of all sexual orientations.

You are a survivor! Although the terms *survivor* and *victim* are used interchangeably in the literature on domestic violence, you have clearly survived a very difficult experience if you're reading this book. This book uses the term *survivor* instead of *victim* exclusively throughout because it feels the most appropriate. Also, research suggests that some individuals who experience a trauma feel that they are a victim first and move into survivorship through the healing process. If this sentiment resonates with you, that's okay, too. It's the goal of this book to move you from feeling powerless into a state of empowerment. In an effort to call abusive behavior what it is, the book also uses terms such as *abuser* and *perpetrator* throughout. Although they may not reflect all that your partner was, these labels are fitting for someone who has inflicted emotional and/or physical harm on another human being. Just as a thief might also be a caring father, an abuser can also be many things; however, we cannot rationalize away an uncomfortable term because of the multiple qualities individuals possess.

As a psychologist working with survivors of domestic violence for over five years, I've heard firsthand how hard it can be to get the necessary support after an abusive relationship. It can be difficult to find a therapist who truly understands domestic violence, and the guilt and shame that exist create a barrier to seeking supportive services. For these reasons, it is my hope that this self-guided workbook will assist survivors in some foundational healing from abusive relationships in a format that is easily accessible.

By picking up this book, you've started your journey toward healing and recovery. You are brave and you are strong. I know that because you're here. In the beginning stages, you may struggle to see the light at the end of the tunnel. I promise you, it is there, just waiting for you. Remember to draw on your innate qualities of dedication and perseverance when things feel overwhelming or pointless. Believe that someday you'll look back on this experience and think, "Wow! I've come so far, and I'm proud of all that I have accomplished."

HOW TO USE THIS BOOK

The content of this workbook is meant to be accessible for someone who's interested in individual healing at their own pace. This book is broken up into eight chapters that have common themes in the healing process for survivors of domestic violence. Within each chapter, you'll find self-guided exercises to help facilitate critical thinking and coping skills. Most chapters begin with a survivor story. Though these stories are fictional, they illustrate common scenarios that survivors experience.

To get the most out of this book, be as honest and thoughtful as possible with your responses to the exercises. If you need extra room to answer some of the questions, feel free to use a notebook. You'll find it helpful to jot down page numbers next to your notebook entries for quick reference.

Some sections may feel harder than others to complete, and that's okay. Because each person's story and journey are different, it's also possible that some sections won't feel relevant to you. Feel free to take as much time as you need for each section, and you may opt to skip around. However, some exercises and content build on previous sections, so you may find some parts difficult to complete without first completing a previous section.

You could also use this book in sessions with a therapist. Similarly, therapists may opt to use exercises in this book for clients if it would be helpful for their healing process; however, it's not intended to be a clinical treatment manual for survivors of domestic violence.

This workbook is intended to provide education on domestic violence and assist with some foundational skills for healing and recovery. Experiencing a trauma can be a harrowing event, and not everyone will heal and recover the same way. For some, this book may be all they need to move forward with a healthier life. For others, this book may only scratch the surface and pave the way toward the desire to do deeper work. If you're in the latter group, therapy can be an excellent modality to assist you with that process. The scope of this book does not include working through any specific diagnosis, such as post-traumatic stress disorder, generalized anxiety disorder, or major depressive disorder, which are all common for survivors of domestic violence.

There is no one right way to facilitate healing and recovery from an abusive relationship. You will heal and move forward in the way that is right for you. Take your time with this book, and if parts of it feel hard, it's okay to skip sections and take breaks. Remember to engage in relaxation and self-care as you embark on this difficult journey. You are resilient, and I know you have the power to overcome this!

CHAPTER 1

understanding domestic violence and recovery

Without awareness there can be no change, so this first chapter begins by helping you gain a greater understanding of what domestic violence is and how it's affected your life. Every survivor's experience is different yet similar in many ways. This chapter will provide you with increased insight into what types of abuse you've survived, dispel common myths, and discuss types of therapy commonly used to help survivors of domestic violence heal and move forward. Welcome to your new beginning.

UNDERSTANDING DOMESTIC VIOLENCE

Domestic violence, also known as intimate partner violence or relational abuse, is a national epidemic affecting 10 million people in the United States annually, according to the National Coalition Against Domestic Violence. Though society conventionally defines domestic violence as a pattern of emotional and/or physical abuse perpetrated by a romantic partner, the term can also include abuse perpetrated by a family member against another family member. National statistics show that approximately 33 percent of women and 25 percent of men have experienced physical violence by a romantic partner in their lifetime. Furthermore, prevalence rates for emotional abuse against men and women are the same, at 50 percent. Given these statistics, it's clear that domestic violence is common in our society and that you are not alone if you've experienced any kind of abusive relationship.

Often, people equate domestic violence with physical violence in a relationship, but the truth is, emotional abuse is also considered domestic violence and can be just as devastating as physical abuse. The "violence" part of "domestic violence" is actually a misnomer because it implies a physical act. Some domestic violence survivors feel that emotional abuse is even more devastating than physical abuse. Have you ever thought, "I wish my partner would just hit me because bruises fade? The mental impact of emotional abuse is forever." If so, you're not alone. Survivors have echoed this statement, in various forms, time and time again.

Domestic violence encompasses a wide array of abusive behaviors rooted in an abuser's desire to maintain power and control in a relationship. Often, people mistakenly attribute abusive behaviors to anger issues; however, anger is really the weapon used to maintain power and control. Abusive behaviors can include physical violence, including sexual assault, and a vast range of other behaviors, such as stalking, gaslighting, name-calling, privacy violations (for example, hacking into email), manipulation, instilling fear, lying, extreme jealousy, false accusations, limiting personal freedom, social isolation, controlling finances, infidelity, threats, intimidation, humiliation, lack of accountability for actions, shifting blame, harassment, and preventing employment.

DISPROVING MYTHS ABOUT DOMESTIC VIOLENCE

Some common myths about domestic violence are that it affects only women, individuals in poverty, and ethnic minorities. Although domestic violence prevalence rates are higher among minority groups, nonminorities also experience domestic violence.

Additionally, the US Department of Justice has reported that individuals in high-income brackets also experience domestic violence, not just those in poverty.

People in heterosexual relationships are not the only ones to experience domestic violence. Same-sex couples also experience domestic violence at similar or higher prevalence rates compared to heterosexual couples. In fact, 43.8 percent of lesbian women and 26 percent of gay men have experienced rape, physical violence, and/or stalking by a partner in their lifetime. Furthermore, individuals who identify as transgender experience higher rates of intimate partner violence than individuals who identify as lesbian or gay. The bottom line: Domestic violence impacts people of all genders, ethnicities, and socio-economic statuses. This book can assist you in healing if you have experienced any form of relationship abuse, regardless of your identity.

THE IMPACT OF DOMESTIC VIOLENCE

Just like each survivor story is different, the impact of domestic violence is different for each person. Suffering more than physical pain, survivors also report a myriad of psychological difficulties that linger after the abuse has ceased. Most commonly, survivors experience feelings of guilt, shame, low self-confidence, low self-esteem, loneliness, a sense of powerlessness, difficulty with independence, sadness, anxiety, fear, and even anger. A lot of people ask, "Now that I'm out of the relationship, why do I still feel so scared/depressed/anxious?" All of these feelings are normal, given what you've been through. Emotional abuse is usually present, in some form, in all abusive relationships, and the psychological impact of this abuse can stay with you long after you leave the abusive relationship. Don't worry! It doesn't have to stay with you forever. By working through your difficulties, you are on the path to living a healthier, happier life.

Let's take a moment to unpack what happens in the body when someone experiences trauma. When we experience an extreme stressor, the nervous system is activated, and the body automatically goes into safety mode by preparing to fight, flight, or freeze. Trauma survivors often report increased heart rate, shallow breathing, face flushing, and/or feeling frozen in place during a traumatic event. Internally, the body is also releasing chemicals such as cortisol, epinephrine, and norepinephrine to assist with the response to fight, flight, or freeze. These biologically hardwired actions are automatic and unconscious. Your body responds in the way that it has quickly determined will provide the highest probability of survival in the face of the threat.

Repeated exposure to stressful events can have a compounding effect on the body's natural fight, flight, or freeze response. When a person is continuously assessing their surroundings for danger, the body's nervous system can get stuck on high alert so that they're prepared when danger arrives. This is a good thing! Your body is doing what it's supposed to do to keep you safe and alive. Now that you're safe from your abusive relationship, you may start to notice that your body is still on high alert. This can result in high anxiety, increased startle response (feeling jumpy or on edge), and/or hypervigilance (sensing danger all the time). Working through your trauma can help settle your nervous system so you'll feel more at ease and safer now that you no longer need to be on high alert.

Identifying Acts of Domestic Violence

Let's take a moment to look over the forms of abuse you survived so we can better understand what you need to heal. Place a check mark next to each one you experienced during your abusive relationship(s). These examples of actions by your partner do not constitute every possibility, so feel free to write in anything you experienced that's not listed here. (In chapter 8, we'll take a look at relationship equality to consider dynamics of healthy relationships for the future.)

EMOTIONAL

- [ ] Denying responsibility for anything
- [ ] Turning blame around on you
- [ ] Waking you up to pick a fight
- [ ] Manipulating you
- [ ] Lying
- [ ] Exhibiting extreme jealousy
- [ ] Demanding perfection
- [ ] Calling the police on you and saying you are the abuser
- [ ] Telling you that you are the abusive one
- [ ] Refusing to speak to you
- [ ] Acting like you aren't present in the room
- [ ] Making threats to scare you
- [ ] Saying things and denying them later

- ☐ Telling you something didn't happen when it did, or vice versa
- ☐ Intimidating you
- ☐ Restricting access to emergency services/police
- ☐ Telling you no one will believe you
- ☐ Refusing you access to your home
- ☐ Threatening suicide
- ☐ Limiting access to your basic needs (food, housing, water, clothing, etc.)
- ☐ Minimizing their abusive actions
- ☐ Not letting you speak during conversations/arguments
- ☐ Minimizing your career/education
- ☐ Refusing to use your preferred gender pronouns
- ☐ Telling you what to wear
- ☐ Other _____
- ☐ Other _____

VERBAL

- ☐ Belittling you
- ☐ Calling you names, like stupid/fat/ugly or similar
- ☐ Screaming at you
- ☐ Body-shaming you
- ☐ Shushing you in public places
- ☐ Teasing you
- ☐ Mocking you
- ☐ Talking over you
- ☐ Other _____
- ☐ Other _____

SOCIAL

- ☐ Restricting your access to friends/family/coworkers
- ☐ Dictating who you can hang out with
- ☐ Monitoring your activities
- ☐ Dictating where you can go
- ☐ Dictating when you can go somewhere

- ☐ Not letting you go places alone
- ☐ Not letting you leave the house
- ☐ Asking you for details about where you have been
- ☐ Denying access to transportation
- ☐ Other _____
- ☐ Other _____

SEXUAL

- ☐ Denying affection
- ☐ Waking you up from sleep for intimacy
- ☐ Pressuring you for sex after you said no
- ☐ Forcing sex
- ☐ Threatening to cheat
- ☐ Cheating
- ☐ Accusing you of cheating
- ☐ Being rough during intimacy without consent
- ☐ Using strangulation during sex without consent
- ☐ Demanding sex as their right
- ☐ Withholding sex
- ☐ Other _____
- ☐ Other _____

PHYSICAL

- ☐ Hitting/kicking/punching/slapping/biting/pinching/strangling
- ☐ Pulling your hair
- ☐ Restraining you
- ☐ Physically stopping you from leaving
- ☐ Spitting on you
- ☐ Blocking the door
- ☐ Throwing things at you
- ☐ Using a weapon
- ☐ Drugging you

- ☐ Other _____
- ☐ Other _____

CULTURAL

- ☐ Isolating you from your culture or the mainstream culture
- ☐ Belittling your culture
- ☐ Mocking your difficulty with language
- ☐ Using language to isolate you
- ☐ Threatening to report you to police/have you deported
- ☐ Refusing to speak in a language you understand
- ☐ Threatening to "out" you to others
- ☐ Using religion to excuse abusive behaviors
- ☐ Denying access to your religious community
- ☐ Other _____
- ☐ Other _____

FINANCIAL

- ☐ Limiting access to money
- ☐ Not allowing you access to the bank account
- ☐ Refusing to let you work
- ☐ Limiting the type of work you're allowed to do
- ☐ Refusing your right to education
- ☐ Controlling the money you spend
- ☐ Making you ask for money
- ☐ Closing your financial accounts
- ☐ Refusing to pay child support
- ☐ Racking up debt in your name
- ☐ Hiding assets from you
- ☐ Dragging out legal battles to drain your finances
- ☐ Other _____
- ☐ Other _____

TECHNOLOGY

☐ Monitoring your email/text communications

☐ Requiring you to turn on location sharing

☐ Installing spy applications on your devices

☐ Sending harassing texts/emails/phone calls

☐ Planting recording devices in your home/car

☐ Stalking you on social media

☐ Monitoring your computer/web searches

☐ Limiting your access to computers/phone

☐ Taking your phone from you

☐ Contacting friends/family to gain access to you

☐ Posting embarrassing images of you on social media

☐ Tracking car mileage

☐ Demanding that you respond to texts/emails/phone calls in a specific amount of time

☐ Demanding that you check in at regular intervals

☐ Other _____

☐ Other _____

CHILDREN/PETS

☐ Threating to hurt the children

☐ Threatening to hurt your pet

☐ Harming a pet

☐ Harming a child

☐ Threatening to take the children away from you

☐ Threatening to take the pets away from you

☐ Belittling you in front of your children

☐ Telling you that you're an incapable parent

☐ Telling you that you're too crazy to take care of the kids

☐ Kidnapping the children

☐ Requiring you to get rid of a pet

☐ Threatening to call child welfare

☐ Other _____

☐ Other _____

Trauma Symptoms

Trauma is often associated with the clinical diagnosis of post-traumatic stress disorder (PTSD); however, not everyone who experiences a traumatic event will meet the criteria for this diagnosis. If you feel you have PTSD, it's best to consult with a licensed mental health professional who can adequately assess your symptoms and provide an accurate diagnosis. Regardless of a formal diagnosis, the impact of relationship abuse can be psychologically devastating for survivors. The following is a list of common trauma symptoms survivors can experience. Look over this list to see what you may be experiencing.

- Lowered self-esteem
- Lowered self-confidence
- Guilt
- Shame
- Self-blame
- Depressed mood
- Suicidal thoughts
- Self-harm behaviors
- Mood swings
- Irritability
- Fatigue
- Difficulty with focus and concentration
- Difficulty sleeping
- Loneliness
- Social isolation
- Restlessness
- Excessive worry
- Panic attacks
- Feeling on edge
- Feeling powerless
- Difficulty advocating for own needs
- Fear of conflict
- Low motivation
- Increased or decreased appetite
- Hypervigilance
- Increased substance use
- Difficulties with trust

- Feeling unsafe in normally safe environments
- Decreased sex drive
- Nightmares
- Dissociation
- Feeling triggered
- Flashbacks
- Avoidance of traumatic reminders (memories, places, people, etc.)
- Feeling detached
- Negative beliefs about the world

TREATMENT

At the core of domestic violence is a power-and-control dynamic, so effective treatment will ultimately help survivors regain power and control in their own lives. When a person experiencing abuse attempts to fight back, whether verbally or physically, the abuser often overpowers them. Over time, survivors learn that standing up for themselves only results in more conflict, so as a safety mechanism, they shut down and no longer advocate for themselves. Helping survivors advocate for themselves again is a crucial component of treatment. As you will see in this book, treatments focus on helping you feel more empowered and less symptomatic and on improving future relationships. Healing for survivors of domestic violence can be achieved using many empirically supported methods, many of which will be implemented in this book. Here are some common types of clinical treatment:

- Modified cognitive behavioral therapy
- Eye movement desensitization and reprocessing (EMDR)
- Somatic experiencing
- Sensorimotor therapy
- Assertiveness and self-advocacy training
- Mindfulness

Treatment is not a one-size-fits-all approach, and therapists will often use a combination of treatment modalities to achieve your goals, just like this book does. Each person's story is unique, so treatment should be tailored to your specific needs. You are the one who is seeking support, and only you know exactly what you need.

A NOTE ABOUT THERAPY

Therapy can be a powerful tool on your path to healing and recovery. Seeking support from a qualified mental health professional can assist you with this process in ways that this workbook cannot. This book is meant to be foundational in the healing process, so the exercises within can help you regain some skills you may have lost during the abusive relationship. This book is not intended to be a workbook for healing trauma, which is a complex process completed with a trauma-focused therapist.

Therapy can help you identify symptoms you may not have noticed, track positive changes in your well-being, and help create a clearer path to healing. Many licensed therapists are trained in the types of clinical treatments previously mentioned, so they can structure a treatment plan precisely for your needs. Individual therapy can also assist you in identifying undesirable patterns in your relationships and how to avoid them in the future.

Furthermore, a therapist will support you on your road to recovery by creating a safe, trusting, nonjudgmental space for you to do deeper work than this book is meant to. Human-to-human acts of trauma can shatter the ability to trust others, which creates difficulties with human connection and relatedness. For this reason, trauma inflicted by other humans, such as domestic violence, warrants targeted treatment that specifically addresses this loss of connection and shattered trust. The therapeutic relationship is a space in which this can be achieved.

Aside from one-to-one therapy, group therapy can be a powerful healing modality for survivors of domestic violence. Abusive relationships often involve tactics that socially isolate you, leaving you feeling guilty, ashamed, and worthless. Working with a group of survivors can help you feel more connected and help you understand that you're not alone. Group therapy can foster trust and belongingness, which have often been broken by the abuse. There may be groups available in your area specifically for survivors of domestic violence. If you're interested in this type of therapy, contact your local domestic violence agency to see if there are any groups in your area.

HOW TO FIND A THERAPIST

Finding a therapist can feel like a daunting task. If you've ever scrolled through one of the many online therapist directories, you know there is an overwhelming number of therapists out there. So, how do you know which one is the right one for you?

Finding a therapist who's skilled at working with survivors of domestic violence isn't just finding someone who specializes in trauma. As mentioned previously, abusive relationships always involve some form of emotional abuse. Emotional abuse is often insidious, and therapists with specific training and experience working with survivors fully understand this. A therapist without specific training in domestic violence may miss key components necessary for the healing process.

When you are searching for a therapist, I highly recommend finding a clinician who has training and experience specifically with domestic violence. They are more likely to understand why it may have taken so long to leave the relationship and how it all has impacted you. Aside from online directories, many communities have domestic violence agencies that offer supportive services to domestic violence survivors. Not all domestic violence agencies will have licensed therapists on staff, but they may be able to recommend someone in your community who is qualified.

In therapy, the relationship between the therapist and the client is everything. Beyond the therapist's specialized training, being able to build a trusting relationship with your therapist is also a key component in the healing process. I recommend looking over a potential therapist's website, if they have one, to get a feel for who they are and what kind of work they do. Additionally, many therapists offer a free consultation during which you can ask questions and get a sense of their style. This is your chance to interview the therapist and see if they feel like someone you might be able to connect with. It's okay to ask questions and it's okay to keep looking if that therapist doesn't feel like the best fit. This is the perfect chance for you to try out some of the self-advocacy skills you will learn in chapter 2 of this book!

"My Dream Therapist"

There are many different types of therapists, so let's take a moment to think about what kind of person you would feel safest with so you can hone in on your dream team. Even if you have been to therapy before, this exercise can still be useful to help you think analytically about who would make a great therapist for you.

1.   Is there a particular gender identity you would prefer to work with?

_____

2. **Are there any healing modalities you feel would work best for you (for example, somatic experiencing or EMDR)?**

_____

3. **What cultural understandings would you like your therapist to have?** Think a bit about aspects of your culture that you value. Culture can include sexual orientation, gender identity, ethnicity, where you grew up, socioeconomic status, language, communication style, and religion/spirituality.

_____

_____

_____

_____

_____

4. **What personality characteristics make you feel safe with a person?** Do they challenge you? Are they down to earth? Do they listen intently? Do they offer you guidance?

_____

_____

_____

_____

_____

5. **What kind of setting feels comfortable to you for therapy?** Maybe it's an office in a high-rise, an agency, a house-like office, or a therapist who will walk with you outside during sessions.

_____

_____

_____

6. **What other qualities would you like in a therapist?**

_____

_____

_____

_____

_____

RECOVERY, RESILIENCE, AND POST-TRAUMATIC GROWTH

There are many words used to identify types of healing from domestic violence in this workbook. What follows is a more in-depth look at what these words really mean and how they can be achieved. At the end of the day, the healing process is all about you and what you want to accomplish. Recovery, resilience, and post-traumatic growth are just a few markers that you may want to incorporate as part of your goals toward a healthier you.

RECOVERY

The word _recovery_ has already come up a lot in this book, but what exactly does it mean? Recovery is the process of returning to a level of functioning that feels good for you. What that looks like will vary from person to person and will largely be dependent on the impact of the abuse. Recovery doesn't necessarily mean that you'll return to your pre-trauma self, and that's okay. Your markers for recovery are the personal goals you would like to achieve to feel better and live a healthier, happier life. In the next exercise, we'll look at what constitutes recovery for you so you can have a road map to success. First, let's talk a little more about some other buzzwords when talking about healing from domestic violence.

RESILIENCE

Resilience is a person's ability to rebound from significant stress and overcome a traumatic experience. Although this may sound similar to recovery, resilience is a trait in humans that fosters recovery. Some research shows that individuals who faced significant stressors during childhood, such as repeated trauma, show lower resiliency levels than those who experienced fewer stressors during childhood. Other research shows that community support, secure attachment to caregivers during childhood, and access to resources can foster higher levels of resiliency. Coping skills are another factor that contributes to resiliency. These skills are tools we use to make ourselves feel better when we experience stress, and they are often learned from our caregivers when we're young. If a child's caregivers have low coping skills for stress, it's likely the child will grow up to also have few coping skills as an adult, leading to low levels of resiliency. So, the more coping skills you have, the greater your resiliency levels are likely to be. Don't worry—if you feel you lack coping skills, this book will assist you with increasing them, helping you rebound from your abusive relationship. Everyone has the capacity to be resilient!

It's probable that you will never again see the world the same way, and returning to a pre-injurious state may feel impossible. Sure, you can find coping skills to assist with anxiety and depression. You can work on trauma processing with a therapist to overcome your abusive relationship. But the truth is, you can't undo the experience of relationship abuse or erase it from your mind. When we experience a traumatic event, it forever changes us, but not all the changes are bad. Yes, there can even be positive growth that comes from experiencing an abusive relationship. Although I never want anyone to experience an abusive relationship, we also need to honor the growth process that exists when we survive something awful.

POST-TRAUMATIC GROWTH

The growth that people experience as a result of trauma is aptly named post-traumatic growth (PTG). In a nutshell, PTG is the positive interpersonal changes a survivor may experience after healing from trauma. The most common areas of PTG are emotional growth, improved life philosophy, increased connection with others, greater life positivity, and engaging in altruistic behaviors. For example, some domestic violence survivors report closer relationships with people who supported them during the abuse. Some who feel brave enough to tell their story to others feel more connected to the community of survivors who come forward to tell them their story. The increase in social connectedness in these two examples would fall under the PTG category of "increased connection with others." This is personal growth that happened as a direct result of experiencing domestic violence. Not everyone experiences PTG during their recovery process. If you don't see any of these changes for yourself over time, that's fine. These are just a few things to keep an eye out for as you work through your difficulties.

Visualizing the New You

I know you want to feel better and live a happier life free from abuse, but what exactly does that look like? How will you know when you've recovered? Because each person's journey is different, let's take a moment to write down your recovery goals so you can have a road map to success.

Sit down, close your eyes, and visualize what your life will look like when you have achieved recovery. In this visualization, think about the following: Who is around you? Who isn't? Where are you? How do you feel? What have you achieved? Then use these images of your future self to answer the following questions. This will help paint a picture of your own personal recovery goals. When you've achieved some (if not all!) of these goals, you'll know that you're on your way to recovery.

1. **What supportive people do you see next to you in this new life?**

_____

_____

_____

2. **Where are you living? Who are you living with?**

_____

_____

_____

3. **How does your body feel?** Think about how your body feels now and what would be different if you felt better. Some examples are feeling less anxious, experiencing better concentration and focus, and feeling emotionally lighter.

_____

_____

_____

_____

4. **What are your new behaviors?** Maybe you're able to walk down the street without constantly glancing over your shoulder. Or maybe you advocate for your own needs more than the needs of others. Feel free to write any changes in behaviors that this new you will embody.

    _____

    _____

    _____

    _____

5. **What will others notice about you when you achieve recovery?** Think about someone talking with you and telling you how you've changed from today. What would this person say?

    _____

    _____

    _____

    _____

6. **What other personal goals have you achieved?**

    _____

    _____

    _____

    _____

SETTING YOURSELF UP FOR SUCCESS

Here are some tips and tricks to help you get the most out of this book. Remember, this is your journey, so go through the book at a pace that feels good for you. If that's once a day, once a week, or even once a month, that's all okay! You've overcome so much already—take it easy on yourself. This is hard work, and it's normal to feel emotional while remembering what you've been through. It's alright to take a breather and come back to these exercises whenever you're ready. Remember, you don't have to complete every section. Although each chapter is intended to build on skills gained in the previous ones, it's fine to skip a section if it feels like it is too much or if it doesn't feel applicable to you. You can always come back to a section later, when you're ready.

If you encounter questions in this book that feel uncomfortable to answer, know that you're on the path to insight. When we sit in uncomfortable spaces, most often we are on the edge of great change. Try to sit with the discomfort for a bit to come up with answers that feel meaningful and new. Not all your answers will feel this way, but the ones that do will level up your healing potential.

Finally, above all, take care of yourself during this process. Know who you can talk to if doing this work feels hard. Engage in self-care and treat yourself with kindness. You are doing good things for yourself by trying to gain a greater understanding of where you've been, what you've been through, and how to avoid these situations again.

CHAPTER 2

empowering yourself

Carmen's Story

Carmen and her former boyfriend, Daniel, dated for five years before she eventually left the relationship. Nothing she did was ever right in his eyes, and he always criticized her for everything—the clothes she wore to the gym, the way she held her wine glass at social functions, the way she cleaned the floors. No matter how many times Carmen tried to change the way she did things to please Daniel, he criticized her anyway. As hurtful as this was for her, Carmen tried everything she could to change her behaviors in an effort to avoid conflict. As she described it, "I felt like I was doing something wrong. I felt like I must be the problem and that I needed to change. I felt like a failure." As Carmen continued to describe her relationship with Daniel, she noted that the verbal arguments were very hard on her. Daniel would become upset at the smallest infraction and get very angry with her. During these arguments, Daniel would yell loudly at her. He would tell her that she's stupid, lazy, and fat. Eventually, Daniel would storm out of the house, slamming the door behind him. When I asked Carmen how she responded to Daniel's anger, she said, "I always tried to make myself as small as possible in hopes that he wouldn't notice me. I apologized profusely for things I never even did, and I did mental flips trying to figure out what I could say to fix the situation." When I asked Carmen if she ever stood up for herself in these scenarios, she said, "I tried in the beginning, but it never worked. In fact, it only made him more irrational and angrier. So I just stopped trying to stick up for myself. I feel so ashamed. I never used to let anyone treat me that way, and I just let him walk all over me."

Although it's been six years since this relationship ended, Carmen finds herself feeling triggered by verbal conflict in other areas of her life. She's now in a healthier relationship with a man who is caring and supportive and communicates fairly. Still, when someone yells at her at work, she instinctively reverts to that person who needs to make themselves small and disappear. Carmen also struggles with advocating for her needs in her current relationship, despite the fairness in the relationship.

ASSESSING YOUR LEVEL OF SELF-ADVOCACY

Advocating for yourself is hard! In our everyday lives, we all have an innate desire to be liked by other people. We often fear that if we go against the grain, others won't like us. When you've experienced domestic abuse, there are several additional factors that contribute to difficulties with self-advocacy. If you attempted to stand up for yourself, you likely found that it increased conflict, and you felt more unsafe. When this happens, your natural reaction is going to be to try something else. In Carmen's story, she tried to stand up for herself, and it only made her abusive partner angrier. Her natural response was to shut down and stop advocating for herself out of fear.

Although Carmen felt shame because she didn't advocate for her needs, her response was actually a really smart one to help her stay safe. Shutting down is a normal safety response to repeated exposure to conflict, especially when you've tried to advocate for yourself in the past and doing so seemingly made the situation worse. Remember our discussion about the body's fight, flight, and freeze modes in chapter 1? Shutting down is an example of freeze mode. Carmen did what she needed to in those moments to stay safe from both emotional and physical harm.

If you experienced anything similar to this in your abusive relationship, you may also have difficulties advocating for your own needs. At one time, shutting down and putting others' needs above yours was self-protective. Now that you're no longer in the abusive relationship, learning (or relearning) how to advocate for yourself is a very important task. Not only will it help you feel more empowered, but it can also assist you with warding off controlling people in the future. Abusers prefer subservient partners they can dominate and control. Hint: If a future partner becomes angry when you try to stand up for yourself, that's a huge red flag. The good news is that the more you practice self-advocacy, the easier it gets. In upcoming sections, we will talk more about how to take back the power that was stolen from you in your relationship. For now, let's take a moment to assess your current self-advocacy skills.

Self-Advocacy Skills

Read this table of common examples of self-advocacy and place a check mark under the column that most closely reflects where you are today for each statement. For the ones that you feel like you've been successful at, be proud of yourself! For the skills you feel could use a little more work, that's okay. Later chapters in this book will help you work on these skills so that you can be an amazing advocate for yourself.

Self-advocacy skills	I do this well	I do this sometimes	I don't do this at all
Using clear communication to have your needs met			
Feeling comfortable talking about your needs with others			
Feeling that your needs are important			
Standing up for yourself when you feel you're being taken advantage of			
Saying no when it's important			
Embracing the possibility of conflict			
Standing tall when someone is getting angry			

Not feeling guilty when you say no to someone			
Doing things because you want to, not because you think you should			
Achieving your personal goals			
Putting your needs in front of someone else's			
Asking for what you need			
Being persistent when it matters			
Not taking on other people's problems as your own			
Setting good boundaries with people and sticking to them			
Doing kind things for yourself			
Engaging in self-care regularly			
Thinking kind things about yourself			
Knowing your self-worth			
Not being apologetic for things you didn't do			

PUTTING YOUR NEEDS FIRST

Healthy relationships are based on equality and effective communication. We will talk more about the hallmarks of healthy relationships in chapter 8, but for now let's consider how getting your own needs met contributes to a healthy relationship. If you're always putting someone else's needs before your own, the playing field is inherently unequal. In these types of scenarios, the giving person is always giving and the receiving person is always receiving. In healthy relationships, each person takes turns being the giver and the receiver.

In abusive relationships, abusers use manipulation, anger, and fear as ways to maintain power and control in the relationship. Have you ever asked for something you needed in the relationship only to have it turned back on you as if you're the problem? In those scenarios, you learned that your needs don't matter and that advocating for your needs creates conflict. For survivors, this can contribute to feelings of fear and hesitancy to advocate for their own needs in the future. Hint: If you're in a relationship and you feel like your needs are not being met, despite your attempts to advocate for yourself, this is a red flag to pay attention to.

It's an admirable trait to do nice things for people and to put your own needs aside sometimes to make someone else happy. Notice I said "sometimes." There can always be too much of a good thing. Putting your needs first doesn't mean you always have to say no to people, but it does mean there's a happy medium between pleasing other people and getting your own needs met. Have you ever said yes to a friend's request to go out to dinner, despite feeling exhausted after work? Once in a while, this is fine, but if you find yourself frequently putting your needs aside for another person out of guilt, then you may be in people-pleasing territory.

Of course, there are situations when staying silent for safety is important, so let's not forget that. If advocating for yourself ever feels dangerous, it's important to follow your gut. Learning to advocate for your needs isn't about putting you in harm's way; it's about assessing the situation to see if it is anxiety or danger that's holding you back. If the latter is the case, always do what feels safest. Your needs matter just as much as someone else's, and advocating for yourself is part of self-care. Believe it or not, sometimes getting your needs met is as easy as just asking!

Assessing Your Needs

If you were silenced over and over again, it only makes sense that you lost your voice. This is your chance to take some power back by understanding what your needs are and how to advocate for them. Take a moment to consider the following prompts and write down goals for how you can advocate for your own needs in your daily life. Often, difficulty with getting your needs met exists in multiple contexts: at work, in friendships, and with family members. Start small—practicing this in a nonrelationship context can help you gain the confidence you need to advocate for your needs when it comes up with a partner in the future.

1. **Think about a few times in your life when you said yes but wished you had said no.** Briefly describe those times here.

_____

_____

_____

_____

_____

2. **Look at your answers to the first prompt to see if there are any common threads.** Do you often have difficulty saying no to new projects at work? Do you often have difficulty declining a social engagement? Do you always say yes to the restaurant your friend picks when you go out to eat, even when you'd prefer something else? Jot down any common threads you notice as you think about your answers from the first prompt.

_____

_____

_____

_____

_____

3. **Thinking about your answers from the previous two prompts, identify which situations feel the easiest for you to try advocating for your needs.** It's important to start with the easiest options and work up to the harder ones.

_____

_____

_____

_____

_____

4. **What are your unmet needs?** They could be emotional, physical, social, or something else. For instance, maybe you're feeling down lately and need support from a friend. Or maybe you've been putting off a dental checkup. Think about your unmet needs and jot them down here.

_____

_____

_____

_____

_____

5. **Thinking about your answers from the previous question, take some time to write down how you could get those needs met.** Maybe you could call a friend and let them know you're feeling down. Or perhaps you could make that dentist appointment you've been meaning to schedule.

_____

_____

_____

_____

6. **Take a moment to think about safe people in your life with whom you might start to advocate for your needs from time to time.** Who are these people?

_____

_____

_____

_____

_____

7. **Now that you've given some thought to this concept in other areas of your life, take a moment to think about your unmet needs in the abusive relationship.** Write down a few times you felt shut down and unable to advocate for your own needs.

_____

_____

_____

_____

_____

8. **Thinking about your answers to the previous prompt, what might you do differently next time?** Remember, there are times when advocating for yourself might not be safe. Those are times when it's okay to be silent. So, in some cases you might not do anything differently, and that's okay, too.

_____

_____

_____

_____

ASSERTIVENESS: YOUR SUPERPOWER

Assertiveness is the skill of being able to stand up for yourself in a calm way without feeling guilty or ashamed. It's also known as boundary setting and goes hand in hand with advocating for your needs. For some, being assertive feels similar to being aggressive, but they're actually different concepts. At times, people can feel guilty or ashamed for being assertive because it means that they're putting their own needs first, and that can feel uncomfortable. Assertiveness is kindly telling someone that the checkout line starts behind you when they cut in line. If you've ever had someone cut in front of you, you may have just let it go. It's not the end of the world. But there are times when we need to be assertive to get our needs met, especially in a healthy relationship. Being assertive helps us feel more empowered, and that's important when you've lost your power to an abusive partner.

Assertiveness is hard for many people and especially for someone who has experienced domestic violence. As mentioned previously, your voice has likely been stifled after advocating for yourself didn't work. Maybe you were once assertive, but now, after the abuse, you feel afraid to stand up for yourself. Or maybe you've always been afraid to stand up for yourself because you were hurt as a child when you attempted to be assertive.

Wherever the fear originated, assertiveness is so difficult for people that there are specific therapeutic interventions called assertiveness training. This type of training empowers people to sit in the optimal space between passivity and aggression to advocate for their needs. Through effective communication skills, you can be assertive—without being aggressive—and advocate for yourself. Imagine not having to wait an extra 10 minutes in line while the person who cut in front of you checks out their entire cart of groceries. Now that's a good feeling!

The New Assertive You

Just like self-advocacy, assertiveness is a form of self-care and a way to set healthy boundaries. Guilt has no place here! It's okay to stand up for yourself—you're worth it. It can feel empowering to stand up for yourself, and others will respect you for doing it.

Communication is the key to assertiveness, so let's take some time to think about how to communicate something that's bothering you. Think about a situation that bothered you in the recent past. Try to think of an instance involving someone who feels safe enough to practice assertive communication skills with. Take a moment to write about this situation. Then, using the concept of assertiveness as explained previously, write out how you might talk to this person about what's bothering you. What would you say? How would you say it? When might be a good time to approach this? What boundaries would you like to set so this situation doesn't happen again in the future?

Self-Defense Classes

Sometimes *feeling* strong is about *being* strong. Learning techniques to physically overpower someone who is twice your size can help you feel both physically and mentally stronger. You'd be surprised at how easy it can be to conquer someone who's much larger than you with a few simple leverage tricks. Taking a self-defense class is a great way to start feeling stronger and more able to take care of yourself if you ever need to. Furthermore, knowing that you have the ability to protect yourself can increase feelings of empowerment and boost self-esteem.

Individuals who practice martial arts regularly report increased strength, improved balance, more self-discipline, and quicker reflexes. Who knows, you may even find a passion for martial arts and make it a new hobby. Plus, it can be the perfect excuse for an outing with friends. There are many organizations that offer free or low-cost self-defense classes, some specifically for women. If this is something you might be interested in, check with your local domestic violence agency to learn if there are classes in your area, or try searching online for classes in your community. I certainly hope you never need to use self-defense skills, but it's better to be prepared in case you ever do.

RECOGNIZING CONTROLLING BEHAVIOR

I've said this already in this book, but it is worth repeating because it's so important. Relationship abuse isn't about anger; it's about power and control. When an abuser is able to take power away from you, it's easier for them to control you. The abuser never has to be vulnerable. Abusers use many tactics to take your power away and maintain control: manipulation, guilt, shame, fear, anger, jealousy, social isolation, and silence. They use all of these awful tricks to maintain power and control in the relationship. Recognizing controlling behavior will help you on your path to healthier relationships. When you notice controlling behavior in someone, you can then use your new superpower of assertiveness to self-advocate.

Andre's Story

Andre and his boyfriend, Jim, were together for almost a year. They met and quickly fell in love. Two months into the relationship, Andre moved in with Jim, at Jim's request. Shortly after they moved in together, their relationship started to change. Jim started accusing Andre of cheating on him, despite Andre's complete fidelity to the relationship. No matter how many times Andre denied the accusations, Jim continued to accuse Andre. Jim had a habit of looking through Andre's text messages and emails and would grill him about innocuous texts to friends. When Jim and Andre were out together, Jim picked fights and accused Andre of looking at other men. In hopes of avoiding conflict, Andre started to avoid going out with friends and kept his eyes toward the ground when the two of them were out in public. Andre felt that Jim loved him and was acting this way because he cared. As the relationship progressed, Jim's behavior became more and more aggressive and accusatory, leaving Andre feeling like he was walking on eggshells.

THE RED FLAGS OF CONTROLLING BEHAVIOR

What forms of controlling behavior do you see in Andre's story? If you quickly noticed extreme jealousy and social isolation as key controlling behaviors by Jim, you're on the fast track to recognizing controlling behavior! But that's not all. There are other insidious controlling behaviors Jim exhibits here. Emotional abuse often incorporates very subtle controlling behaviors. Once you know what they are, you can watch out for them in your own relationships.

Let's take a closer look at Andre's story. Andre moved in with Jim very quickly after the relationship began. Abusive relationships often feel like a whirlwind and progress very quickly. This is a huge red flag. Abusers often ask their partner to move in early in the relationship and often propose marriage prematurely. The abuser has more access and more control when you're cohabiting because they can watch you more closely.

If you remember, Jim also picked random fights with Andre regularly, another red flag. Jim used the controlling behavior of unjustifiable anger to keep Andre subservient. Feeling like you're walking on eggshells trying not to upset your partner is yet another red flag. Never knowing when the next outburst will happen, survivors adapt their behaviors to appease the abuser. Somehow, this never seems to work. The abuser still finds irrational things to get angry about, which leaves you feeling like nothing you do is right. Truthfully, nothing you did was wrong. You tried your hardest to make someone you love happy.

An abusive partner will find something to get angry about, no matter how you change your behavior. Finding someone who accepts you for who you are is possible. We'll talk more about how to achieve a healthy relationship in chapter 8. For now, let's assess the types of controlling behaviors you experienced in your past relationship(s).

Watching Out for Controlling Behavior

Let's go back to the checklist you completed in chapter 1, Identifying Acts of Domestic Violence (page 4). Take a moment to look over your answers. Each of the abusive behaviors listed in that exercise is a controlling behavior. In the abusive relationship, what abusive behaviors did you notice early on but ignore or rationalize away? List these red flags here so you can watch out for them the next time they pop up in a relationship.

1. _____

2. _____

3. _____

4. _____

5. _____

6. _____

7. _____

8. _____

9. _____

10. _____

"BUT I'M SUPPOSED TO . . ."

Growing up, we learn that there are certain cultural expectations we're "supposed to" adhere to. Have you ever thought any of the following?

- But I'm supposed to make the marriage work until death do us part.
- But I'm supposed to make my partner happy in the bedroom.
- But I'm supposed to be the strong one in the relationship.
- But I'm supposed to be skinny/muscular.
- But I'm supposed to cook and clean for my partner.
- But I'm supposed to be nice and not argue.
- But I'm supposed to pretend that everything is okay.

We've learned from society that these are things we're expected to do and need to do in life. These "supposed to" statements make us feel guilty and ashamed if we don't or can't live up to them. These types of beliefs can keep us from living happy, fulfilling lives. Not only that, but they can also keep us in an unhealthy relationship because we think we "should" stay. We'll talk more about the pitfalls of "should" statements in chapter 6, but for now let's think more about what you actually want to do versus what you think you're supposed to do.

Have you ever stopped to ask yourself, "What do I actually want to do?" One of the keys to happiness is living your life authentically. Authenticity involves allowing yourself to be yourself without feeling guilt or shame for being who you are. Fear of being judged often holds us back from being authentic. The world is full of people telling us what we are supposed to do. If we decide to go against these social expectations, we fear being ostracized. Do you know anyone who lives life authentically—someone who spends their life setting personal goals and obtaining them, without fear of what others might think of them? If you do, you have a great role model to help you visualize how to live your life authentically. Making decisions based on what you think you're supposed to do can leave you feeling unfulfilled and resentful that you're not doing what you actually want to do.

"But I Want to . . ."

Take a moment to relax, close your eyes, and imagine what life would be like if there were no judgment. Sit and think for a moment: What would it feel like to be living in a world where no one judged you, and no one told you what you're supposed to do? You could do and say anything and be anyone you wanted. There are no barriers to what you want to achieve. Everything is possible! Next, try to answer the following questions.

1.   **How would your life be different than it is now?**

_____

_____

_____

_____

_____

_____

2.   **Where do you see yourself?**

_____

_____

_____

_____

_____

_____

3.   **Who do you see yourself with?**

_____

_____

_____

_____

_____

_____

4. What emotions are you feeling in this visualization? What does it feel like in your body?

_____

_____

_____

_____

_____

_____

5. What accomplishments will you have achieved?

_____

_____

_____

_____

_____

_____

6. Now, think about your current reality. What "supposed to" statements are holding you back from achieving this vision?

_____

_____

_____

_____

_____

_____

7. **What can you do now to live your life more authentically?**

_____

_____

_____

_____

_____

_____

What Have You Learned?

Journaling is the process of writing out your thoughts as they come to you. When journaling, there's no need to write perfectly or spell everything correctly. This process is only for you, so try not to feel self-conscious about what you write. No one has to read it but you. This process will help you get your thoughts down on paper, which will make it easier to reference and review later if you feel the need. For some, writing down their thoughts can help create meaningful, deeper connections with the subject matter.

Now that you've completed chapters 1 and 2, take a moment to think about what you learned. Then use the space provided to journal your thoughts. You may like to explore any or all of these questions: What knowledge have you gained here? What changes would you like to make to improve your life? How will you incorporate assertiveness? How will you set boundaries with others? What are the markers of controlling behavior you want to watch out for?

_____

_____

_____

_____

_____

_____

_____

_____

_____

_____

_____

_____

_____

_____

QUICK TIPS FOR SELF-EMPOWERMENT

Remind yourself it's okay to do any of the following:

- Say no.
- Stand up for yourself.
- Set boundaries with people.
- Put yourself first.
- Ask for what you want/need.
- Speak up.

CHAPTER TAKEAWAYS

- Self-advocacy is about putting your own needs first when necessary.
- It's healthy to put your needs first at times, even when it feels uncomfortable to do so.
- Being assertive isn't the same as being aggressive. It's about using your voice to get your own needs met.
- Power and control, not anger, are at the root of abusive behavior.
- One key to happiness is living your life authentically, and that means not allowing others to dictate what you "should" be doing.

CHAPTER 3

letting go of guilt and shame

Veronica's Story

Veronica and her former partner, Ben, dated for four years. They met at a local coffee shop where Veronica worked. In the beginning, Ben was the perfect partner. He doted on her, bought her lavish gifts, was kind to her two children, and helped her financially when she was in need.

After living together for about a year, Ben started getting physically abusive. The first time he slapped her, Veronica was shocked and told Ben that if he ever did that again, she would call the police. He mocked her and told her that no one would believe her. The next day, Ben apologized profusely for his aggressive outburst and told Veronica that it would never happen again. He bought her flowers and got takeout from her favorite restaurant that evening. Veronica believed that he was sorry and decided to give him another chance.

But over time, Ben became more and more physically abusive. The slapping turned into punching, and he became very controlling. Ben started using her phone to monitor her location on a regular basis and dictated who she could spend time with. After every abusive outburst, Ben emphatically apologized for his anger and did kind things for Veronica to say he was "sorry." Veronica talked with her friends and family less and less because of the conflict with Ben. She didn't want anyone to know what was happening in their relationship, so she kept silent about the abuse.

Veronica thought that she had to maintain the image of a happy family and felt embarrassed. Plus, Ben often threatened to harm the children if she told anyone. She thought that if she could just change her behavior, he wouldn't get so angry with her and things would get better. Additionally, Veronica believed that Ben would change and stop being abusive, as he said so many times. Unfortunately, the abuse only became more frequent, and Veronica eventually took her two children and left.

But even after she left, Veronica still felt so ashamed, and because of that, she didn't tell many people what happened. She worried that no one would believe her, just as Ben said, and blamed herself for not being able to make things right. She also felt sorry for Ben. She knew he had "anger issues," yet she felt guilty that she left him all alone. She blamed herself for letting the abuse go on as long as it had and expressed guilt about putting her children in that situation. As she looked back on the relationship, she wondered, "Why didn't I leave him sooner? I should have known better."

THE GUILT MONSTER

Feeling guilt and shame both during and following an abusive relationship is quite common for survivors. These two words—*guilt* and *shame*—are often used in conjunction because shame can foster guilt and, conversely, guilt can foster shame. Sure, you can have one without the other, but they often hang out together in the mind.

Guilt is the nagging feeling that you've done something wrong or haven't done something you "should" be doing. It's behavior oriented and sometimes is actually a good thing. Feeling guilty can propel us to act differently and do something more in line with our values. Guilt can help us live more authentically if we act on our feelings of guilt to change what is making us feel guilty.

When we consider Veronica's story, we understand that her guilt in response to the impact of the abusive relationship on her children likely fueled some of her desire to leave. If that's true, Veronica's guilt helped motivate her to leave her abuser, and that's amazing! However, in the case of domestic violence, guilt does not usually serve such a productive purpose. Abusers use feelings of guilt to their advantage to keep you from leaving the relationship. They play on your high levels of empathy by suggesting that you've done something wrong and should therefore feel guilty. Even after you leave the relationship, those implanted feelings of guilt may still linger.

Analyzing Your Guilt

Let's take a look to see how much the guilt monster might be impacting your overall well-being. Circle the number that most closely corresponds to your response to each of the situations. When you're finished, add up your total for each column, and then calculate your overall total to see how much guilt you might be holding on to.

Statement	Not at all likely	Somewhat likely	Highly likely
You wake up in the morning with a headache, runny nose, and cough, so you decide to call in sick to work. How likely are you to feel like you should be at work because you are letting down your coworkers and/or boss?	0	2	3
After you've had a hard day at work, a friend calls you and asks you to come over and help them move a piece of furniture. You kindly say no, not today. How likely are you to spend the rest of the evening feeling like you should have said yes?	0	2	3
You're at a family member's house, and you bump into a bookshelf. A glass figurine falls to the ground and breaks. Your family member says it's no big deal. How likely are you to spend the rest of the evening apologizing for your mistake?	0	2	3
You are off work for the day and spend the day watching TV. You realize it's 5 p.m. and you're still in your pajamas. How likely are you to feel like you should have done something more productive with your day?	0	2	3
You move to an area that has harsh winters, and you realize you don't have any winter boots. You spend some of your savings on a new pair of boots to keep your feet warm and dry. How likely are you to feel like you spent too much each time you put them on?	0	2	3
Totals			

Overall Total:

Mild Feelings of Guilt: 0–4 points

Moderate Feelings of Guilt: 5–9 points

Excessive Feelings of Guilt: 10–15 points

THE SHAME MONSTER

Shame can seem similar to guilt, but it has some poignant differences. Shame is focused on the self instead of on behavior. Shame is feeling like we aren't good enough and that we are bad. Shame correlates with depression, anxiety, substance abuse, and eating disorders, which means people with high levels of shame also have a high likelihood of experiencing some or all of these difficulties. Learning to understand that your actions were not shameful is an important step in the recovery process. Staying in an unhealthy relationship does not mean you're bad, and you don't deserve to be judged because someone harmed you.

Please understand that the abuser is responsible for their actions, which cannot be rationalized away by being empathetic for their situation. Many people get angry, have mental health issues, or engage in substance abuse. These same people are not necessarily abusive to their partners. Given this, we cannot say that someone is abusive because they drink too much or are having a rough time at work. People abuse because they are abusive, not because of some other factor. The only person who should feel ashamed is your abuser.

Analyzing Your Shame

Let's look to see how much the shame monster might be impacting your overall well-being. Circle the number that most closely corresponds to your response to each of the following statements. When you're finished, add up your total for each column, and then calculate your overall total to see how much shame you might be holding on to.

Statement	Not at all true	Somewhat true	Very true
I feel like I'm not good enough.	0	2	3
I feel like I can't do anything right.	0	2	3
There must be something wrong with me.	0	2	3
Nobody really likes me.	0	2	3
I'm not as smart as other people.	0	2	3
Totals			

Overall Total:

Mild Feelings of Shame: 0–4 points

Moderate Feelings of Shame: 5–9 points

Excessive Feelings of Shame: 10–15 points

OVERCOMING GUILTY AND SHAME-BASED THINKING

In the context of your abusive relationship, you might have believed that you were responsible for hurting your abusive partner. You may have put this blame on yourself, or you may have been manipulated into thinking you were to blame. Either way, guilt such as this creates shame. Although guilt can propel us to do something more in line with our values (such as make amends), it also can immobilize us. The latter serves no healthy purpose. Don't let your abuser live in your head rent-free.

There are times when we feel guilty or ashamed about something; however, when we think more logically about it, we come to understand that we actually didn't do anything wrong. For example, have you ever felt guilty about turning down a social invite because you were too tired? In this example, you've decided that your needs are less important than the other person's and that you caused them harm. You decided that your exhaustion is second to someone else's need to socialize with you.

Let's apply some critical thinking to this example. Have you ever had someone turn down an invitation to spend time with you because they were too tired/stressed/busy? If yes, would you have wanted them to come out despite their emotional state? Would you have preferred that they suffer through it to spend time with you? Did you feel like they owed you an apology for declining your offer? I'm going to go out on a limb here and assume that you answered no to the last two questions. As an empathetic person, you probably wouldn't want someone else to suffer. So if all this rings true for you, then why would it be harmful when you say no? Why should you feel guilt or shame?

Sometimes guilt and shame are the result of catastrophizing. Catastrophizing happens when we overgeneralize situations and blame ourselves. For instance, saying something like this is catastrophizing: "I'm such a terrible friend because I forgot my friend's birthday." Basically, this statement says that you're always a terrible friend because you forgot someone's birthday once. Do you always forget birthdays? Is there a time when you didn't? Does missing one birthday make you a horrible friend to everyone? Answering these questions can help you think more analytically about the original statement and help you see that even though you made a mistake, that does not actually equate to being a terrible friend to everyone you know.

Goodbye to the Guilt and Shame Monsters

Take a moment to think about an occasion from the recent past when you felt guilty or ashamed about something. Answer the following questions about this event.

1. **What was the situation surrounding the guilty or ashamed feeling?**

_____

_____

_____

_____

_____

2. **Is the feeling that comes up related to guilt, or shame?**

_____

3. **What is the statement you made to yourself that induced guilt or shame?**

_____

_____

_____

_____

4. **What evidence do you have that this statement is true?**

_____

_____

_____

_____

5. What evidence do you have that this statement is untrue?

_____

_____

_____

_____

_____

6. Is this statement always true? If not, why not?

_____

_____

_____

_____

_____

7. Would you think someone else should feel guilty or ashamed if they were in the situation instead of you? Why or why not?

_____

_____

_____

_____

_____

8. Are you using catastrophizing in this situation? Why or why not does the statement qualify as catastrophizing?

_____

_____

_____

_____

_____

9. Is there something you can do to make amends or learn from this situation moving forward?

_____

_____

_____

_____

_____

10. After considering all these questions, how do you feel about this event now?

_____

_____

_____

_____

_____

There are five main types of guilt that people experience. Each type of guilt can lead to shame.

- Guilt for something you did
- Guilt for something you didn't do, but want to
- Guilt for something you *think* you did
- Guilt that you didn't do enough to help someone
- Guilt that you're doing better than someone else

In many cases of guilt resulting from an abusive relationship, that guilt may actually stem from someone manipulating you into thinking that you're guilty for something. Using guilt to manipulate is a form of emotional abuse that can stay with you long after the relationship ends. With each of these types of guilt, the key is to think analytically about where the guilt came from and to assess whether or not you actually did something that was hurtful to someone. If you didn't, releasing the guilt is about being kinder to yourself by squashing your inner critic. If you did, releasing that guilt often means making amends; however, it is usually not in your best interests to reach out to an abusive ex to make amends. This could be detrimental to your well-being and suggest to the abuser that you're willing to reengage with them.

BREAKING THE SILENCE

Guilt and shame fuel silence, as was the case with Veronica. Abusers prey on these emotions and often use them to their advantage to keep you in the relationship. When we think back to Veronica's story, we can see that she felt embarrassed about the abuse and hid it from everyone in her life. Her silence, although understandable, allowed the abuse to continue in secrecy. When there is silence, there can be no change. Abusers need to be held accountable for their actions, and breaking the silence can sometimes foster accountability.

Additionally, breaking the silence allows survivors to get support from others, which is a critical component of the healing process and often essential in making a safe exit plan. Studies have shown that breaking the silence can provide support, validation, and foster trust, which all promote recovery. If you've broken the silence with even one person, you are on your way toward healing and support. Breaking the silence happens each time you talk to someone new about your abusive experience. With each disclosure, you may find yourself feeling more and more comfortable talking about what happened to you. Also, remember that silence may be required for safety. There are certainly times when remaining silent is necessary so that you avoid harm. In those moments, know that your silence is important and may save your life.

HINDSIGHT IS 20/20

Have you ever looked back on something you said or did and thought, "I should have done x, y, and z instead"? I'm guessing you said yes, because pretty much everyone has experienced this thought at some point in their life. Evaluating our actions and words after the fact can help us learn from our experiences, which is a great thing! Through this process, we can become smarter and more adept at navigating similar situations in the future. For instance, if you look back on your abusive relationship and think, "I could have stood up for myself in the beginning," that's a great thought and a teaching moment. You now have the knowledge that standing up for yourself early on could help set firm boundaries in future relationships.

Unfortunately, time machines don't exist. There's no way to know what you know now and go back and change something you did or said. If we start to worry and shame ourselves for our past mistakes, instead of learning from them and moving on, we're in self-criticizing territory.

Common phrases such as "I should have known better" or "I knew this would happen" come to mind in these types of situations. Truthfully, you did the best you could at that time, and now you know more, so you can make better decisions in the future. If you find that you're worrying and shaming yourself about things that you cannot delete from the past, the key is to turn it into a teachable moment for yourself so you can learn and move forward. Getting down on yourself because you wish you had done something differently is unhelpful and serves no healthy purpose. When you learn from your past and are kind to yourself about it, you can then move forward as the wiser person you are.

HINDSIGHT BIAS

Hindsight bias is the false belief that you could have predicted the outcome of an event before it ever even happened. In research studies, low relationship satisfaction has been linked to increased levels of hindsight bias. This means that the more dissatisfied you are with a past relationship, the higher the likelihood that you feel you should have known better. You're probably at least somewhat dissatisfied with your previous abusive relationship. Inherent to hindsight bias is the idea that you knew something would happen but failed to prevent it. Unless you have special powers, you cannot predict the future, so there's no way you could have prevented something from happening. Again, this type of thinking serves no healthy purpose.

Hindsight bias only makes you feel small, unwise, and not good enough. Remember the story of Veronica at the beginning of this chapter? As she thought back on her relationship with Ben, she felt that she should have known better and should have left sooner. There's that hindsight bias creeping up for her. Veronica felt that she could have prevented the abuse by knowing what she knows now but didn't know then. Veronica didn't know that Ben was going to become abusive, because she could not predict the future.

Learning from the Past

Take a moment to think about a time when you said, "I should have . . . ." We're going to use it to shift your perspective from statements that make you feel like you somehow fell short of expectations to ones that you can learn and move forward from. Let's hold off on the statement "I should have left sooner," because we're going to address that biggie in the next section. Try to find a different situation in which you felt like you should have known better or wish you had done something differently. Write your "should" statement in the left column. Then use the space next to your statement to write what you learned from experience.

I should have . . .	I learned that . . .

"I SHOULD HAVE LEFT SOONER"

If you've ever thought that you should have left the abusive relationship sooner, then this section will resonate with you. Survivors of domestic violence say these words quite often, so you're not alone. If we look back again at Veronica's story, we see she expressed guilt and shame because she felt she "should have left sooner." Veronica dismissed the fact that she had good reasons to stay in the relationship, despite the abuse. Ben threatened to harm her children, and she stayed, in part, out of fear for the well-being of her kids. She also stayed because she loved him, and she believed that he could change.

There are many reasons people stay in an abusive relationship for longer than they feel they should. Love and fear are just two of them. It's important to remember that you stayed in the abusive relationship for a reason, maybe even more than one reason. You made the decisions that were best for you in those moments, and we have to honor your wisdom at that time. You left when the time was right for you. The following are a few common reasons survivors stay in abusive relationships longer than they would like. Do any of these resonate with you?

- Love
- Fear of deportation
- Reluctance to leave the children alone with the abuser
- Being afraid the abuser will take the children away permanently
- Fear of being socially ostracized by family and/or society
- Fear of harm or death
- Low self-esteem
- Lack of financial means for an exit
- Lack of employment
- Language barriers
- Shame and guilt
- Hoping the abuse will stop
- Hoping the abuser will change
- Believing the abuse is your fault
- Believing separation from either parent would be emotionally harmful to the children
- Cultural beliefs that separation/divorce is not an option

JEKYLL AND HYDE

The book *The Strange Case of Dr. Jekyll and Mr. Hyde* is the story of a man who drinks a potion and transforms from a kind, sweet gentleman (Dr. Jekyll) into a nasty, violent man (Mr. Hyde). Did you ever feel like your partner was both Jekyll and Hyde? If you said yes, you're not alone. Many survivors feel that their abusive partner has a dichotomous personality of sweetness and rage. "It's like he's a totally different person when he gets angry." This statement is almost as common as "I should have left sooner."

The sweet, caring, kind, generous, attentive partner is the one who keeps you invested in the relationship. It's often a significant reason survivors stay, despite the abuse. Feeling like your partner will be able to maintain the sweet version, someday, is enough to keep you trying to make it work. Survivors don't want the relationship to end; they just want the abuse to stop. Unfortunately, it's very rare that the abuse stops over time. Most often, it only gets worse.

"I Could Have Left Sooner, but . . ."

If you've ever thought you should have left sooner, let's take a moment to consider your reasons for staying. Understanding why you stayed can help decrease the guilt and shame you may feel for maintaining the relationship as long as you did. If it's helpful, you can refer to the previous list of common reasons to complete some or all the following sentences. You can use a piece of paper if you'd like to complete more.

1. **I could have left sooner, but I didn't because I . . .**

   _____

   _____

2. **I could have left sooner, but I didn't because I . . .**

   _____

   _____

3. **I could have left sooner, but I didn't because I . . .**

   _____

   _____

4. **I could have left sooner, but I didn't because I . . .**

   _____

   _____

5. **I could have left sooner, but I didn't because I . . .**

   _____

   _____

What Have You Learned?

Now that you've completed chapter 3, let's take a moment to think about what you learned. Use the space provided to journal your thoughts about what knowledge you gained here and what changes you'd like to make to improve your life. You may like to write about the following topics: How will you shut down unhelpful guilt and shame? What fortune-telling statements will you change? What mistakes do you want to learn from?

QUICK TIPS AND STRATEGIES TO HANDLE GUILT AND SHAME

Here are some quick tips to remind you how to handle guilt and shame when they creep up:

- Think analytically.
- Think of alternative perspectives.
- Engage in self-compassion.
- Remember that you're a good person.
- Turn the guilt into a learning exercise for yourself.
- Make amends, if it feels safe to do so.
- Let the guilt go.

CHAPTER TAKEAWAYS

- As a result of the abuse, feelings of guilt and shame are common for survivors of domestic violence.
- Guilt is feeling as if you've done something wrong, whereas shame is feeling as if you're somehow not good enough.
- The key to getting over guilt and shame is to notice the often irrational thoughts they elicit and engage with them in a more rational way.
- Breaking the silence about your abuse is an important part of the healing process that happens every time you tell someone new about your abuse.
- Survivors stay in abusive relationships longer than they would like for a variety of understandable reasons.
- You can't change the past; however, you can learn from your mistakes and move forward.

CHAPTER 4

handling stress and anxiety

Jo's Story

A few days before our meeting, Jo went to the hospital because she was having chest pains and trouble breathing. The doctors ran some tests, but everything came back normal. The doctors told her they couldn't find anything physical and said that her discomfort was likely a panic attack. They recommended that she see a therapist to help her cope with her anxiety. Sure, she experienced anxiety in the past, but recently it had increased. She started having trouble concentrating at work, and she became concerned that she might lose her job due to poor performance.

During the therapy intake session, Jo noted that she often felt restless, had trouble falling and staying asleep at night, felt irritable, and couldn't stop worrying about things in her life. She said, "It's like my brain just won't shut up. When I lie down to sleep, I lie there for hours thinking of all kinds of things." When I asked Jo about recent stressors in her life, she disclosed that she just got out of a "toxic" relationship with her now ex-girlfriend. As she described the relationship, she reported feeling like she was "walking on eggshells" during that time. Her former partner was extremely jealous and accused her of sleeping with anyone she interacted with. During the last argument they had before Jo finally left for good, her ex-girlfriend had accused her of infidelity and pushed her down the stairs. Jo made an exit plan the following day and moved out of their shared home while her former partner was at work. Since then, Jo has felt extremely anxious and unsettled.

ANXIETY AND TRAUMA

Believe it or not, anxiety is actually a functional, hardwired biological response to stress. Yep, I said it: Anxiety is normal. Let's say you encounter a snake in the wild—there's a high likelihood that you'd stop walking and freeze as you assess what to do next. That reaction is anxiety, and it's a normal response to stress. When we humans encounter an actual threat to safety, our nervous system spikes, and we get anxious. It's part of that fight, flight, or freeze response discussed in chapter 1. This anxiety creates a desire to avoid the anxiety-provoking situation—like spotting a snake—and get to safety.

If anxiety is normal, then why does it get so out of control? Well, once again, there can always be too much of a good thing. You may experience a spike in anxiety because you're afraid you might fail a test. This anxiety may propel you to study harder for the test so you have a better chance of passing. That's a great way to harness anxiety for the better. On the other hand, if you have so much anxiety about the test that you avoid thinking about it at all and don't study, that's not a good thing. Although you've avoided some anxiety-provoking stimuli, you will eventually have to face the test, and you might not do so well. This latter example may create more anxiety the next time you have a test, because you didn't do so well the previous time.

Anxiety is often a symptom of trauma, meaning that the root of anxiety is sometimes unresolved trauma. If you've been in an abusive relationship, anxiety may be one of the symptoms you experience. Living in an environment where it felt like nothing you did was ever right or walking on eggshells because you never knew when the next angry outburst would come from creates anxiety. In those moments, your body is always evaluating the environment for danger as a safety mechanism. Because your nervous system is constantly on high alert, your body experiences anxiety. As explained in chapter 1, your nervous system can get stuck in "on" mode and have difficulty settling back to a calm, non-anxious state. Other environmental stressors can compound and create high levels of anxiety and also panic attacks. In Jo's story, we understand that her previous abusive relationship, coupled with other environmental stressors, led to heightened anxiety and panic attacks. Jo's anxiety eventually lessened over time through awareness, coping skills, and stress management techniques.

Assessing Your Anxiety

Take a moment to look over this anxiety symptom chart to see if you could be experiencing anxiety. This exercise isn't meant to diagnose an anxiety disorder; it's meant only to help you understand if you experience anxiety so we can help you minimize any symptoms. If you experience high levels of anxiety, please contact a licensed mental health professional.

Over the past month, how often have you experienced the following symptoms?

Daily or almost daily = 2 points each

At least a few times per week = 1 point each

Never = 0 points each

Once you've completed this self-assessment, find your score according to the instructions.

Anxiety symptoms	Daily or almost daily	At least a few times per week	Never
Trouble falling asleep at night			
Trouble staying asleep at night			
Difficulty staying focused			
Excessive worry that you find difficult to control			
Difficulty relaxing			
Feeling restless			
Increased irritability			
Staying busy so you don't have to sit with your thoughts			
Feeling fatigued			
Increased heart rate			
Dizziness/feeling faint			
Trouble breathing			
Gastrointestinal issues			
Feeling overwhelmed			
Having increased muscle tension			
Experiencing frequent headaches			
TOTALS			

Now, tally your results for each column and add them together for a total score. Then use the answer key to learn about your individual anxiety.

Answer Key
Very Low Anxiety: 0–4 points
Mild Anxiety: 4–10 points
Moderate Anxiety: 11–21 points
High Anxiety: 22–34 points

ENVIRONMENTAL STRESSORS

Environmental stressors are anything in your environment that contributes to higher stress levels. In the case of Jo, her job loss concern is an environmental stressor that's contributing to her heightened anxiety. Things like living in poverty, toxic work environments, getting a high tax bill, and loss of a loved one are all examples of environmental stressors. They are anything in our immediate day-to-day life that adversely impacts our overall well-being.

Leaving an abusive relationship is an inherently stressful event. It often means that many major adjustments need to happen to make a safe and successful exit. For many survivors, their life changes dramatically after leaving an abusive partner, and their environmental stressors increase even as they rid themselves of the toxic relationship. The following are some common stressors associated with leaving an abusive relationship:

- Financial concerns
- Housing worries
- Employment concerns
- Grief due to relationship loss
- Relocation
- Concerns regarding the welfare of children
- Navigating a single-parent household
- Childcare
- Pet care
- Dealing with continued harassment/abuse from the ex
- Feeling unsafe
- Lack of or low social support

- Dealing with mental health issues
- Divorce proceedings
- Custody negotiations

Beyond all the exit stressors, daily life also has stressful moments to throw on top of it all. Maybe your car broke down recently, or your child was reprimanded at school for misbehaving. Whatever the stressor, the compounding effect of multiple stressors can be difficult to manage, especially when you're trying to make a new life for yourself, free from abuse.

Combating Stress and Anxiety

Mindfulness is the art of staying focused on the present and is one of the most powerful interventions for stress and anxiety because it relaxes your mind. The most important trick to managing anxiety and stress is to remember that you can't be anxious and relaxed at the same time. It's just not physically possible. Given this, the key to managing stress is to increase relaxation. To practice mindfulness, take a moment to notice where you're sitting and respond to the following prompts:

- Where are you?
- Describe what the space looks like.
- What does the space feel like?
- What is the temperature of the space?
- Where are the exits?
- What do you see/smell/hear/taste/touch?
- As you look around the space, what catches your eye?
- Find something in the room that feels calming or peaceful to look at for a few seconds.
- Allow yourself to focus on this calming thing in the room.
- When you're ready, take another look around the room.
- After completing this exercise, notice how your body feels and take a moment to put your thoughts into writing.

_____

_____

_____

_____

_____

_____

_____

_____

_____

_____

_____

ESCAPE AND AVOIDANCE

As discussed earlier in this chapter, humans have a natural tendency to avoid distressing stimuli. If you see a snake, you're likely to avoid it because it could be harmful. In the future, you may avoid taking that path again because you saw the snake there previously. Seems smart, right? In a relationship where you experienced abuse, you probably learned to avoid certain things in an effort to increase safety and decrease conflict. That was also very smart. Now that the relationship is over, you may find yourself continuing to engage in these avoidance tactics, despite the fact that they're no longer necessary. What was once a helpful coping skill can become a hindrance once it doesn't serve a purpose anymore. This happens because you developed a new way of being in the world to adapt and survive the abusive relationship. At the time, you experienced relief from distress through avoidance.

You may find that you have a tendency to avoid difficult thoughts and feelings, as well. If this is the case for you, that's also using avoidance to relieve emotional distress. Unfortunately, when it comes to our emotional pain, we actually have to sit in it for it to dissipate. Thus, avoiding distressing memories can actually hinder your healing process. You have to go _through_ it; you cannot go _around_ it. If we stuff down our feelings and memories, the distress relief is short term. Over the long term, the unprocessed stress compounds, much like anxiety, and can result in difficulties living your life the way you want to.

Avoidance Tactics

Now that we've talked about what escape and avoidance mean, let's take a moment to think about what kinds of things you notice yourself avoiding. These things may be memories, people, places, activities, or something else. Write down each one you think of. (In the next section, we'll talk more about how to handle these distressing events as they come up for you.)

1. _____

_____

2. _____

_____

3. _____

_____

4. _____

_____

5. _____

_____

6. _____

_____

7. _____

_____

8. _____

_____

9. _____

_____

10. _____

_____

HANDLING TRIGGERS

A trigger is something that would normally be innocuous but reminds you of a traumatic event when you experience it. Triggers can be people, places, events, sights, sounds, sensations, tastes, smells, specific words, colors, a song, and more. For instance, you may find yourself feeling frightened if someone at the grocery store gets irritable with a checkout clerk. If during your abusive relationship your partner's irritability was a sign that something bad was about to happen, you may feel scared or anxious when someone in your environment is irritable. Triggers make you feel like you're in danger, even when you're not.

When someone experiences a trigger, it can feel reminiscent of the traumatic event and engage the stress response in your nervous system. Another example could be the smell of a particular cologne or perfume. If your abusive partner wore a specific scent, you may feel triggered if you smell that scent while walking by a stranger. You might see images of your abusive partner in your mind, look around to see if that person is there, and realize, thankfully, they are not.

Think back to Carmen's story in chapter 2. She experienced verbal abuse in her relationship. Even though the abusive relationship ended many years ago, she finds herself feeling anxious and frightened at work when a coworker is irritable. Irritability in and of itself isn't a dangerous event to witness. Mostly, people get irritable and then later calm down, without harming another person. But Carmen's instinctive reaction is to try and make herself as small as possible, similar to her response to her abusive partner's anger. Although the two situations are vastly different, irritability is triggering for Carmen and results in her feeling like she's back in an abusive relationship for a moment.

Often, when a survivor feels triggered, they'll use avoidance to cope with the triggering stimulus. Think back to the example of someone being triggered by a perfume scent. This person might then avoid ever going into the perfume department at a store. Though avoidance allows for relief of discomfort over the short term, it can create difficulties over the long term. The goal is to know what your triggers are and work through them so you can uncouple the trauma response from normally innocuous stimuli. Enacting some coping skills can combat mild triggers. However, for more moderate to severe triggers, you may experience panic and engage in a full fight, flight, or freeze response. If this is the case for you, working through your triggers is best facilitated with a licensed mental health professional who can support you along the way.

Identifying Your Triggers

Let's take a moment to journal about your own triggers so we can then practice some grounding techniques to help you when you experience a trigger. This exercise has three parts.

1. What situations feel triggering for you? What happens in your body when you experience a trigger? What could you try the next time you feel triggered? Sometimes even just thinking about your triggers can be triggering. Remember to engage in self-care if you need to during this exercise.

_____

_____

_____

_____

_____

_____

_____

_____

_____

_____

2. Now that you have a better understanding of what kinds of situations you feel triggered by, let's talk about ways to help you through these triggers. Grounding techniques are a form of mindfulness that helps us center ourselves. The most common grounding technique is to sit in a chair or on a couch and allow both feet to touch the ground. Try sitting on something that allows you to comfortably have both feet on the ground. As you do this, notice what it feels like to have your feet planted this way. You can also notice how it feels to have your back supported by what you're sitting on. Stay with these thoughts for a moment and allow your body to relax. By doing this, you're literally grounding yourself.

3. Some other common grounding techniques are to do any of the following:

- Name five colors around the room
- Pay attention to your breathing
- Touch an item near you and notice how it feels
- Count a repetitive object in your environment (e.g., ceiling tiles or trees)

Try a few of these techniques. Remember to take note of how your body feels afterward, and then journal about your experience.

_____

_____

_____

_____

_____

_____

_____

_____

Turning Triggers into Tiny Ants

Triggers can come on suddenly and leave you feeling disoriented and unsafe. They don't have to hold you back from living a full and complete life. You can overcome this instinctive response by facing your triggers and implementing coping skills. The following are tips to help you calm yourself when you feel triggered.

- Remind yourself that you are now safe.
- Remind yourself that this situation is different from the abusive one.
- Engage in relaxation techniques to calm your nervous system.
- If possible, seek support from someone near you.
- Scan the area for exits so you can leave if you need to.
- Remove yourself from the trigger if it becomes too overwhelming.

ASSESSING LOSSES

During the course of your abusive relationship, you may feel you lost pleasure in things that you previously enjoyed. For instance, maybe you used to enjoy cooking prior to the abuse. During the relationship, your abusive partner criticized your cooking and hovered over you to rush you to finish. This created anxiety and fear that you would do something wrong. After experiencing that over and over again, you have a high likelihood of experiencing fear and anxiety while cooking for yourself, even after your abuser is long gone. You might rush through cooking dinner for yourself, or you might avoid cooking altogether. The love you had for cooking may feel lost, but you wish you could enjoy it again. The good news is you can! You can feel joy again for the things you previously relished. In the next section, we'll talk a little more about how to do this by decreasing avoidance due to fear and anxiety. For now, let's do an exercise to help you understand what you feel like you lost during the abusive relationship.

"Things I Miss . . ."

Let's take a moment to think about what kinds of things you miss because fear and/or anxiety are keeping you from them. These things may be people, places, activities, or something else. Write down each one you think of. (In the next section, we'll talk more about how to decrease avoidance of these things.)

1. _____

   _____

2. _____

   _____

3. _____

   _____

4. _____

   _____

5. _____

_____

6. _____

_____

7. _____

_____

8. _____

_____

9. _____

_____

10. _____

_____

LETTING GO OF AVOIDANCE HABITS

Learning to face your anxiety and fear is an important part of the process of healing from an abusive relationship, but this should be done only if it's safe to do. For instance, if you feel fearful of your abusive ex-partner, and you avoid places where that person might be, that's not something you want to stop doing. The things you might want to stop avoiding are things that will help you live a healthier and happier life.

The opposite of avoidance is engagement—meaning that in order to stop avoiding anxiety-producing things, you'll need to actively engage with them. Now, this isn't necessarily a one-step process in which you just do the thing that you're avoiding. This can be done gradually by working up to facing your fears.

Let's look back at the example of avoidance of cooking. The trick to learning to love cooking again is to relax while engaging in cooking. You cannot be relaxed and anxious at the same time—it's just not possible. Someone who avoids cooking altogether might want to start small and practice simultaneous engagement and relaxation by just going to the grocery store and buying a few items to cook for a snack. Eventually they would work their way up to cooking a larger meal, once they've mastered making smaller snacks and meals without feeling activated. A step-by-step plan for working through avoidance in this type of situation might look like this:

1. Engage in a grounding or relaxation exercise prior to starting this task.
2. Remind yourself that you're safe and that cooking is not inherently an unsafe task.
3. Make a grocery list.
4. Check in with yourself to see if you feel anxious. (If you do, engage in a grounding or relaxation exercise.)
5. Drive to the grocery store and park.
6. Check in with yourself to see if you feel anxious. (If you do, engage in a grounding or relaxation exercise.)
7. Proceed into the grocery store and again remind yourself that you're safe.
8. Check in with yourself to see if you feel anxious. (If you do, engage in a grounding or relaxation exercise.)
9. Shop for the necessary ingredients.
10. Get back in your car.
11. Check in with yourself to see if you feel anxious. (If you do, engage in a grounding or relaxation exercise.)
12. Drive home.
13. Put the groceries away.
14. Check in with yourself to see if you feel anxious. (If you do, engage in a grounding or relaxation exercise.)
15. Congratulate yourself on succeeding in the first step of conquering your avoidance!

As you can see from this example, the key to success with conquering avoidance is checking in with yourself regularly to see if you need to engage in some self-care. With repeated successes such as this, the anxiety is replaced with a new response: relaxation. You're effectively retraining your brain to find the thing you've been avoiding to now be relaxing and enjoyable instead of anxiety producing.

This book is intended to assist you only with mild situations of avoidance. If certain trauma stimuli invoke a feeling of panic and feel too difficult to manage on your own, it's best that you seek professional mental health services to assist you in combating these difficulties. Remember to take all the time you need to complete these exercises, and do them only if you feel it would be helpful in your healing process.

Combating Avoidance

Let's put what you just learned about anxiety and avoidance to the test. Look back at your answers to the previous exercise about the things you miss, and pick one of them that feels easiest to tackle. Create a step-by-step guide for yourself on how you could reengage to face your fears and anxiety. You can use the cooking example to help you structure yours in a similar manner. If you need more space, feel free to use a blank sheet of paper for extra steps.

Step 1: _____

Step 2: _____

Step 3: _____

Step 4: _____

Step 5: _____

Step 6: _____

Step 7: _____

Step 8: _____

Step 9: _____

Step 10: _____

What Have You Learned?

Now that you've completed chapter 4, let's take a moment to think about what you learned. Use the space provided to journal your thoughts about what knowledge you gained here and what changes you'd like to make to improve your life. Here are some questions you may like to explore: What types of anxiety and stress do you experience? What will you do to combat these? What are your avoidance tactics and how will you face them better moving forward? What triggers do you have and how would you like to manage them?

_____

_____

_____

_____

_____

_____

_____

_____

_____

_____

_____

_____

_____

QUICK TIPS AND STRATEGIES TO HANDLE STRESS AND ANXIETY

Stress and anxiety are a normal part of life. Here are a few quick tips to help you handle stress and anxiety:

- Practice calming techniques regularly when you're not stressed.
- Check in with yourself regularly to see if you're feeling stressed or anxious.
- Get active regularly to decrease compounding of stress and anxiety.
- Name the emotion you're feeling.
- Relax yourself before going into a stressful situation.
- Engage in regular self-care.
- Stay in the present.

CHAPTER TAKEAWAYS

- Anxiety and depression can be symptoms of underlying trauma, such as experiencing an abusive relationship.
- Environmental stressors can adversely impact mental health, leading to feelings of stress and anxiety.
- Relaxation and mindfulness are two helpful tricks to combat stress and anxiety.
- Some helpful avoidance tactics you may have developed during the abusive relationship may not serve you well over the long term.
- Triggers are stressful stimuli in the environment that remind you of a traumatic event, even though the situation is actually different.
- Grounding techniques are helpful in combating triggers when they come on.
- You may find that you don't enjoy certain things as much as you once did because of the abusive relationship. You can find joy in these things again with some practice and patience.

CHAPTER 5

releasing anger

Miriam's Story

Miriam felt full of guilt and shame after having an affair one time. She met her husband in college, they had four children, and they had been married for 25 years. Up until a year ago, her husband was the only person she'd ever been with. Her husband found out about the affair and was very angry with her. After he found out, he installed tracking devices on her phone, monitored her phone calls, and regularly checked her email and text messages for anything he might find incriminating, all without her consent. Additionally, he began demanding sex from her nightly. Often, she would wake up in the middle of the night to find him on top of her, and if she said no, he pressured her even more. She would eventually give in just to get it over with. Although she felt personally violated for the physical and privacy intrusions, Miriam often said, "I deserve it. He cares about me, and I should pay for what I did to him."

In our first few therapy sessions, Miriam often looked at the floor and cried a lot. Over time, Miriam's mood began to shift from sadness and guilt to anger and outrage. She gained a greater understanding that what she was experiencing was considered domestic violence and that she had the power to stand up for herself. She started setting firm boundaries with her husband and not backing down. She changed her password for her phone and computer and refused to give in when he demanded sex. Miriam's shift from guilt and shame to anger was the powerful moment when she decided that she deserved to be treated better, regardless of the infidelity. Through her anger, she gained the power to fight back in a healthy way. Eventually her anger propelled her to leave the abusive relationship and move forward to live a happier life.

ANGER AS A SECONDARY EMOTION

Secondary emotions are emotions that are triggered by another, primary emotion. Anger, while still valid, is often a secondary emotion. For instance, if you feel angry because someone forgot to invite you to a birthday party, you may feel unimportant, which spurs anger. So, in this example, feeling unimportant is the primary emotion and anger is the secondary emotion. Anger is often used as a defense mechanism to hide vulnerable feelings that feel too uncomfortable to share.

For survivors of domestic violence, anger can be a powerful tool for change. However, if anger is the only conscious feeling, it can also mask primary emotions, thereby hindering the healing process. Being emotionally in tune means being able to recognize, and hold space for, multiple emotions that come up simultaneously. For instance, you may continue to feel sadness, anger, love, and betrayal toward your abusive ex-partner long after you've left. Domestic violence survivors often experience anger toward their past partner, the justice system, social services, family, and other people and systems. All of these feelings are valid, and they all deserve acceptance and attention.

Understanding Your Emotions

Let's take a moment to tap into any anger you might have to see what's underneath. If your first thought is that you don't have any anger, I encourage you to remember that everyone feels angry at times, and that it's okay to feel that way. Use the spaces provided to write down what you feel angry about. Then think about what emotions could be underneath the anger and write those down, too. Some of the common feelings hiding under anger are hurt, fear, sadness, guilt, shame, and betrayal.

1. **I feel angry because . . .**

_____

_____

What are the primary emotions under this anger?

_____

_____

_____

2. I feel angry because . . .

_____

_____

What are the primary emotions under this anger?

_____

_____

_____

3. I feel angry because . . .

_____

_____

What are the primary emotions under this anger?

_____

_____

_____

4. I feel angry because . . .

_____

_____

What are the primary emotions under this anger?

_____

_____

_____

5. I feel angry because . . .

_____

_____

What are the primary emotions under this anger?

_____

_____

_____

IS ANGER EVER HELPFUL?

Yes! Humans have a spectrum of emotions and all of them are valid—even anger. When we swear off anger as a bad emotion, we shut off a very human part of ourselves. We simply need to be angry sometimes. It's how we deal with our emotions, including anger, that is the key to living a healthy life. Suppressed anger can lead to emotional outbursts, resentment, and depression. Just like anxiety and stress, anger compounds and can become a ticking time bomb if you don't find an outlet for it. Plus, it can take years off your life. We'll talk more about that later, though.

Think about Miriam's story at the beginning of this chapter. Her anger propelled her to make some changes that helped her advocate for herself and eventually leave the relationship. Now that's anger I can fully support. An example of reacting in an unhealthy way would be if Miriam's anger resulted in her engaging in a physical altercation with someone. (This would be an unhealthy response, unless it were in self-defense.) When first involved in therapy for domestic abuse, the survivor is usually withdrawn, guilt-ridden, ashamed, and accommodating. When anger begins to surface, it's a joyful moment in the therapy process because it means that the survivor is on the cusp of great change. Many survivors feel guilt and shame when they start to feel angry at their abuser, so if you've felt like that, know that it's completely normal.

"How Anger Has Helped Me"

Take a moment to think about situations in your life when anger may have been helpful for you. Why was the anger helpful? What changes did you make because of anger?

_____

_____

_____

_____

_____

_____

_____

_____

_____

_____

_____

ANGER AND YOUR HEALTH

Although anger is a valid emotion, too much of it can lead to a host of health problems. We often see our emotions as existing only in our brain, but research shows that our emotions can actually impact our physical well-being, too. Chronic anger has been linked with increased risk of heart disease, high blood pressure, anxiety, depression, sleep difficulties, and frequent headaches.

Chronic anger can also adversely impact our relationships with others. Though you may try to bottle up the anger, others can often sense underlying anger and hostility and be wary of spending time with you. Suppressed anger can also make you less likely to spend time with others and make you feel irritated with loved ones for small infractions. Acting out your chronic anger can result in feelings of guilt and shame for behaving in such a way. It can even impact your performance at work, creating difficulty with focus and concentration. But don't worry if you feel angry. Anger doesn't have to rule your life. Next, we'll talk about ways to manage and let go of unhelpful anger.

Combating Unhelpful Anger

Progressive muscle relaxation is a technique that lets you tune in to your body by tensing and relaxing your muscles from head to toe. This can help you relax and release unhelpful anger when you feel it come up. To practice this technique, begin by sitting in a comfortable position. Then start with the first body part on the list and move down the list until you reach the last one. Tense and release each muscle group for 10 seconds at a time. Note how you feel once you've completed this exercise.

- Forehead
- Mouth/lips
- Jaw
- Neck
- Shoulders
- Arms
- Wrists
- Hands
- Stomach
- Buttocks
- Legs
- Ankles
- Feet
- Toes

After completing this exercise, my body feels . . .

_____

_____

_____

_____

FUNNELING YOUR ANGER TOWARD RECOVERY

As we've briefly discussed, anger is a healthy part of the healing process. Anger can help motivate us to create change. It's also an emotion that exists to facilitate the fight, flight, or freeze safety mechanism we're biologically hardwired for. This means anger may have been part of your motivation to leave your abusive relationship. Depending on where you are in your healing process, you may not have tapped into your anger yet, or maybe you're just starting to feel twinges of anger. Either way, harnessing your anger to promote healing is a healthy part of moving forward. Some people may feel frightened by anger if it starts to surface. It's alright to feel angry about something. It's what you do with this anger that matters the most. It's not okay to take your anger out on others, but it's okay to feel angry and sit with that emotion when it comes up.

Anger to Motivate You

Let's take a look again at your answers to the first exercise in this chapter, Understanding Your Emotions (page 70). Use the space provided to discuss ways you can harness this anger to motivate you to change. For example, maybe you feel angry that your abusive partner tainted your love of cooking by criticizing your cooking process or the foods you prepared. You can use your anger to decide that you will learn to love cooking again.

1. **I can use my anger to motivate me to . . .**

   _____

   _____

2. **I can use my anger to motivate me to . . .**

   _____

   _____

3. **I can use my anger to motivate me to . . .**

   _____

   _____

4. **I can use my anger to motivate me to . . .**

_____

_____

5. **I can use my anger to motivate me to . . .**

_____

_____

TRAUMA AND MOOD SWINGS

It's normal to experience changes in mood throughout the day or week. However, in the aftermath of an abusive relationship, domestic violence survivors often report mood shifts that occur out of nowhere. Moods can change from intense sadness to irritability to numbness to hopelessness, all in a matter of hours. Trauma-related mood swings are the result of nervous system dysregulation (caused by fear, fight/flight/freeze, or hypervigilance) due to continually sensing danger in your environment. Most often, mood swings feel out of proportion to the situation, leaving you feeling guilty and ashamed for feeling that way.

Mood swings are a signal that you need some self-care. The trick is to take a moment to identify the emotion you're feeling and think about how you can take care of yourself in that moment. Here are some ways you can deal with mood swings if they affect you:

- Name the emotion you're feeling and say it out loud.
- Tell yourself it's okay to be angry from time to time.
- Go for a walk or take a few deep breaths.
- Recognize that you're not in danger.
- Remove yourself from the triggering situation.
- Use grounding techniques.
- Apologize if your mood impacted someone else.
- Talk with someone about how you're feeling.
- Practice a relaxation skill.
- Watch a funny movie or stand-up comedy show.

My Mood

Over the next week, use this mood tracker to help you identify instances of mood swings. Each time you experience a mood swing, write down what happened, how you felt, what the triggering event was, and how you handled it. At the end of the week, look at your log and see what coping skills were most helpful for you. Also note any common themes that come up. By creating a toolbox of coping skills, you can then use these skills whenever you feel your mood start to shift.

Event	Identified mood	Triggering event	Coping skill

STRATEGIES TO LET GO

Now that we've talked about ways that anger can be both helpful and hurtful, let's take a moment to discuss what you can do if you feel unhelpful anger. Generally, feelings of anger will dissipate fairly quickly. But if you find yourself ruminating on your anger, it's time to shift your mind-set into a more positive space. At times when we feel angry, we tend to blame others for our emotional reaction. Unfortunately, we cannot blame others for our feelings, because they are ours and ours alone. No one can make us feel anything. You have the power to decide how you react to something and how it affects your mood. You can choose to be angry about something, and you can also choose to not let it affect you.

Letting go of your anger so you can move forward can feel hard at first, but with practice, it gets easier. The first step is to identify what emotion may be underneath the anger, as we talked about earlier. Once you've done that, here are a few tips to help you let go of unhelpful anger:

- Remind yourself that what angered you is in the past, and being angry cannot change it.
- Tell yourself that ruminating on your anger isn't helpful.
- Find another outlet to express your anger, such as creating art, exercising, or screaming into a pillow.
- Remember that you are in control of your emotions, not someone else.
- Use your anger to motivate you toward change.
- Use grounding or relaxation techniques.
- Engage in mindfulness.
- Talk it out with someone close to you.

Letting Go

Think about how you might let go of something that makes you angry. This could be a current situation that you feel angered by or something that has come up in the past. What have you done in the past to help you get rid of anger? What new skills for decreasing anger do you think you might try? What are the benefits of letting go of your anger?

_____

_____

_____

_____

_____

_____

_____

_____

_____

_____

_____

_____

_____

Laughter Therapy

Humor can be a powerful tool to decrease feelings of irritability, stress, and depression. Just as with anxiety and relaxation, you can't feel happy and irritable at the same time. Laughter therapy is a form of stress relief that can work to combat anger and irritability. Not only can laughter help you cope with life stressors, but also laughter boosts neurochemicals called endorphins, creating a calming effect. Furthermore, laughter has been shown to boost your immune system, lower stress hormones, and prevent heart disease.

Laughter therapy is easy to practice on your own, wherever you are. To do this, start by smiling and then progress to pretend laughter. If you can think of something funny to start off this process, that can also be helpful, but it's not necessary. You can create fake laughter and that often will eventually turn into real laughter. This process can feel weird at first. If you find that it's difficult to turn the pretend laughter into real laughter, that's okay. Simulated laughter has been found to have the exact same benefits as real laughter. The more you practice this skill, the easier it gets.

What Have You Learned?

Now that you've completed chapter 5, let's take a moment to think about what you learned. Use the space provided to journal your thoughts about what knowledge you gained here and what changes you'd like to make to improve your life. What healthy anger do you have?

Do you experience chronic anger, and if so, what can you do about it? How can you calm yourself when you feel overly angry?

_____

_____

_____

_____

_____

_____

_____

_____

_____

_____

QUICK TIPS AND STRATEGIES FOR EMBRACING YOUR ANGER

- Don't suppress your anger; allow it to come out in a healthy way.
- Remember that anger is a valid emotion.
- Use anger to help motivate you toward change.
- Recognize what emotion is underneath your anger.
- Remember that everyone experiences anger from time to time.
- Be kind to yourself when you experience anger.

CHAPTER TAKEAWAYS

- Anger and irritability are common feelings for survivors of domestic violence.
- Feeling angry isn't always bad, but too much anger can have a negative impact on your well-being.
- The key to healing is understanding what emotion is at the root of anger.
- Anger can be an amazing motivator for healthy change.
- Mood swings are a common symptom of trauma you can work through.
- Practicing simulated laughter can help combat anger and relieve stress.

CHAPTER 6

changing how you talk to yourself

Isabelle's Story

Isabelle met her former partner, Cat, while working at a ski resort. Cat was spending the winter skiing and the two of them quickly hit it off, spending the entire winter together. Isabelle was attracted to Cat's adventurous nature and generosity. Cat was quite wealthy and took Isabelle out for lavish dinners, surprised her with jewelry, and told Isabelle that she had never met another woman as beautiful as her. Isabelle thought she had met the woman of her dreams—smart, funny, kind, and attentive. After dating for several months, Cat began "teasing" Isabelle about her nondesigner clothing and telling her that she was embarrassed to take her to parties because of her clothes. Soon, hurtful comments from Cat became the norm instead of the occasional "joke." If Isabelle made a mistake, Cat would say that it was because Isabelle was uneducated and stupid. If Isabelle had a rough day at work, Cat would tell her that maybe she should find another job because she would never amount to anything as a ski instructor anyway. If they went out together in public, Cat would comment on other women's appearance and say, "Look at how beautiful she is. You should work out more so you can be that thin."

Isabelle really wanted Cat to admire her, so she tried as hard as she could to keep up with Cat's expectations, but it seemed that nothing she did mattered. The insults just continued, and Isabelle started to believe that she, herself, was the problem, like Cat said. One night, Isabelle was upset and crying and Cat mocked her, calling her a baby. As if that weren't hurtful enough, Cat began yelling at Isabelle as she cried, calling Isabelle worthless and accusing her of crying just to get attention. She started to believe that no one would ever love her as much as Cat. Isabelle spent a lot of time thinking about ways to make herself more attractive so Cat would treat her well again. Deep down inside, Isabelle felt like a stupid, worthless person who deserved all the insults Cat hurled at her. She started to feel depressed, and on the worst of days, she could barely find the motivation to get out of bed.

BEING KIND TO YOURSELF

It's no surprise that after leaving an abusive relationship, survivors often experience lowered self-esteem and express feelings of worthlessness, just like Isabelle. When someone is told that they are smart and competent over and over again, they start to believe it. Similarly, when someone is repeatedly told that they're stupid and ugly, they start to believe it.

But just because someone makes an assessment of you doesn't mean it's true. If you're like many other survivors, you may have internalized hurtful messages from your abuser as the truth. You may feel like you were the problem in the relationship and that you just weren't good enough for your ex-partner. Learning to love yourself again takes time. It takes repeated messages of self-love to get you back to knowing that you're an amazing person with amazing qualities, even with all your flaws. You have the power to increase your self-confidence and sense of self-worth.

Many times, when we talk down to ourselves, we say things that we would never say to or even think about other people. Additionally, when you talk to yourself negatively, it has the same mental impact as if someone else were saying these things to you. This is harmful to your well-being and can lead to lowered self-esteem, lowered self-confidence, depression, anxiety, and social isolation. Negative self-talk also includes being overly apologetic. Do you find yourself apologizing for things that you don't really need to apologize for? If so, you may do this out of guilt, shame, or anxiety, but not because you truly feel you have done something wrong.

Combating Negative Self-Talk

If you find yourself talking down to yourself, it can be helpful to monitor your thoughts and learn how to talk to yourself in a kinder voice. To complete this exercise, you'll monitor your thoughts for a few days to a week and note the times when you have a negative thought about yourself. Write down what the situation was and what negative things you said to yourself. Then explore what's beneath these thoughts. To do this, ask yourself the following questions:

- Is this thought really or always true about myself?
- What evidence do I have for this thought?
- What evidence do I have against this thought?
- If I asked a friend if this is true about myself, would they agree or disagree?
- Are there times in my life when I'm the opposite of this thought (like smart versus stupid)?
- How could I reframe this thought to be more positive about myself?

After you think about each of these questions, use the space provided to jot down how you can reframe this thought into something more positive about yourself. If you practice this, over time, it will become easier for you to notice your negative thoughts and reframe them for yourself on the fly.

Situation that happened	Automatic negative thought	Positive reframing

"SHOULD HAVE" AND "COULD HAVE"

Life is full of shoulds: I should have left sooner. I should have stood up for myself. I should feel better by now. If you've ever said any of these things to yourself, you're should-ing yourself. And you're probably not the only one. People love to give unsolicited advice and tell us what we "should" be doing.

How we talk to ourselves has a huge impact on our mental health and well-being. Let's take a moment to think more analytically about the word *should*. It has a critical and shaming context that we are not doing something we are supposed to. This often leads to guilt and shame that we are somehow not living up to our fullest potential. The truth is, you could be doing things differently, but you don't have to. If you replace the shaming word *should* with *could*, then the meaning of a sentence changes drastically. Consider the following example:

> *I should have left sooner.*
> *I could have left sooner.*

Take a moment to think about how the meaning of these seemingly similar sentences changes because of one word. The sentence with *should* feels shameful—like you were to blame for something you weren't doing. In the second sentence, *could* intrinsically implies that you were making a choice and that there was a reason behind this choice. Changing the way you talk to yourself isn't just about reminding yourself that you're amazing. It's also about choosing words that accurately convey the intended meaning.

Changing *Should* to *Could*

Let's take a moment to think about some "should" statements that you notice yourself making. Write them out on the lines. Then take that same sentence and replace the *should* with *could*. After you do this, think about how the new sentence feels compared to the old one. Which one feels better to you? After you complete this exercise, try to replace "should" statements with "could" statements when you talk to others and yourself.

I should have . . .

_____

_____

I could have . . .

_____

_____

I should have . . .

_____

_____

I could have . . .

_____

_____

I should have . . .

_____

_____

I could have . . .

_____

_____

I should be . . .

_____

_____

I could be . . .

_____

_____

I should be . . .

_____

_____

I could be . . .

_____

_____

I should be . . .

_____

_____

I could be . . .

_____

_____

"WHY?"

Have you ever wondered, "Why did this happen to me?" The question of "why" comes up frequently for survivors of abuse. When a person experiences a traumatic event, it can shatter their view of the world as a safe and just place. This leaves many survivors wondering why bad things happen to good people and results in attempts to extrapolate meaning from traumatic chaos.

Understanding Your Whys

What whys do you ask yourself? Are these questions helpful to you? Are you blaming yourself unnecessarily for things? Is it possible to move forward without answers to these "why" questions? If yes, how will you do that? Use the space provided to try to answer these questions for yourself.

LEAVING THE PAST IN THE PAST

Do you ever find yourself stuck thinking about the past and wishing you could go back and change things? Unfortunately, there's no way to change what happened in the past. After experiencing abuse, you may find yourself spending a lot of time wondering why this happened or what you could have done to prevent it. It's no easy task to put our difficult experiences behind us, especially when those experiences involved being hurt by another person. Putting the past in the past doesn't mean that you have to forgive or forget what happened. It means that you make a conscious choice to move forward and not get stuck dwelling on the past.

Think about this statement: Depression is all about the past, and anxiety is all about the future. This means that people who spend a lot of time worrying about the past are likely to experience a depressed mood. Similarly, people who spend a lot of time worrying about the future are likely to experience anxiety. If we stay in the present, we have neither of those things. It's time to leave your past where it belongs—in the past—and move forward into the present. Thinking about the past can help us learn from mistakes and move forward, but if you find yourself getting stuck there, it may hinder your healing process. Using mindfulness is a great way to halt those thoughts of the past that you get stuck thinking about.

When you feel yourself start to drift to thoughts of the past that are unhelpful, use the following techniques to try switching gears in your brain. Take note of which ones feel the most supportive for you so you can use them the next time you need them.

- Ask yourself, "Are these thoughts helpful for me?"
- Tell yourself that you want to leave these things in the past so you can move forward.
- Remind yourself that you cannot change the past, so it's unhelpful to continue to think about it.
- Bring yourself back into your environment by looking around you and noticing something calming around you.
- Put on a song you love and listen intently to the lyrics.
- Focus on your breathing.
- Imagine yourself putting the thought of the past into a box, closing the lid, and placing the box behind you, knowing that you can access it at any time in the future if you want to.

Putting Your Thoughts Behind You

Sometimes, the same unhelpful thought of the past pops up over and over again. Most everyone has experienced this at some point in their life. The goal of this exercise is to put the thought away in a space for safekeeping so you don't have to hold it in your head any longer. With this helpful trick, you can package away those stubborn thoughts or memories that nag at you. For this exercise, you'll need a container with a lid and something to write with. Use the space provided below to write a draft of two or three recurring thoughts of the past. Then copy those thoughts to separate scraps of paper and fold them up so they fit in the container. Place the lid on the container and put the "thought jar" somewhere out of the way for safekeeping. In the future, when these thoughts creep back into your mind, remind yourself that you've written them down and tucked them away, so there's no need to keep reviewing them in your head.

1. _____
   _____
   _____
   _____
   _____

2. _____
   _____
   _____
   _____
   _____

3. _____
   _____
   _____
   _____
   _____

FEELING SAFE VERSUS FEELING UNSAFE

Do you feel safe? Although the word *safe* doesn't name an actual emotion, we use it often to describe a state of psychological well-being. To be more accurate, we could rephrase this and ask, Do you feel psychologically safe? To feel safe is to feel calm and free from possible harm in your immediate environment. Survivors of domestic violence often don't feel safe in their surroundings, even when the environment poses no actual threat to safety. This is due to the trauma symptom of hypervigilance that we mentioned earlier in the book.

When you experience real threats to your safety on a regular basis, your body gets stuck in the "on" mode, making you hyperaware of any possible danger in the environment. Being hyperaware means that you can react quickly and get yourself to safety if you need to. At some point, this hypervigilance may have been a helpful coping mechanism to keep you safe. However, you may find that long after the abuse has ceased, you continue to feel on edge or unsafe, even though this is no longer necessary. Additionally, being hyperaware means that a person can perceive something innocuous as a threat and react to it.

Let's consider the following case example.

> *Jeffery is a survivor whose ex-husband ushered him out of a gas station at knifepoint (unbeknownst to the people around). Following this, Jeffery was severely beaten by his abuser and spent two weeks in the hospital. Two years later, Jeffery has ended the relationship and no longer sees his abuser; however, he refuses to go to a gas station and seeks assistance from friends to fill up his car with gas. For Jeffery, getting gas feels unsafe. Does this seem logical? Probably not, because generally gas stations aren't dangerous places. Let's add that Jeffery's abuser doesn't know where he lives and is currently incarcerated. There is no danger of Jeffery's abuser showing up at a gas station in his town, and the probability that he will be attacked in a gas station is very low. Despite knowing this, Jeffery continues to engage in safety-seeking behaviors because they make him feel safer.*

As a result of abuse, survivors of domestic violence use safety-seeking behaviors, even if logic says they don't need to. You've likely adapted and found some coping mechanisms for yourself, but some of these adaptations may not be healthy over the long term. In Jeffery's case, he now asks friends to help when his car needs gas, or he takes public transportation because it feels safer than going to a gas station. Even just thinking about going to a gas station increases Jeffery's anxiety.

Safety-seeking behaviors are generally not present prior to the traumatic event, and these behaviors change the way the survivor engages with the world. It's worth noting that there are many cases in which feeling unsafe is accurate and real due to possible threats in your environment. You may have very good reason to feel unsafe, such as if your abuser is continuing to stalk you, and doing things to increase your safety is actually a good thing. It's important to determine if feeling unsafe is logical or not, because actual safety is a number one priority for survivors.

"How I Feel Unsafe"

Have you ever noticed yourself doing something to make yourself feel safer after the abuse? Let's take a moment to list common situations where you feel unsafe and the safety-seeking behaviors you use to compensate with. (In the next exercise, we will talk more about coping skills you can use to feel safer in these situations, maybe even without your safety-seeking behaviors.)

I feel unsafe when . . .	To help myself feel safer, I . . .

Feeling unsafe in your environment can be extremely stressful. There are many ways to combat the stress and help you feel calmer, such as the guided visualization exercise on page 93. Here are more coping skills that you can try when you find yourself feeling unsafe in what would ordinarily be a safe place:

- Scan the room you're in and notice the exits. Remind yourself that you know where they are if you need them for any reason.
- Tell yourself you're safe. Though this might sound silly, reminding yourself that you are safe can actually help you feel safe.
- Move to another place in the room or area that feels safer. Sometimes just moving to another side of a room or standing next to someone you know can help you feel safer.
- Remind yourself that the situation you're experiencing in the present is not the same as the traumatic situation you were once in.
- Take a moment to feel your feet connecting to the ground.
- Notice how your body is feeling as you feel unsafe. Are you tensing a part of your body? If so, use your mind to relax that part of your body that feels tense or stiff.

TRAUMATIC LINKS

Let's think again about Jeffery's story. He identified the gas station as a contributing factor in the abusive attack. If we break this thought apart more analytically, we see that the gas station did not harm Jeffery. His abuser harmed him. The actual threat to his safety was being in close proximity to his abuser. In this example, Jeffery "overcoupled" gas stations with fear. Overcoupling happens when someone experiences a traumatic event and the mind then links together two things that aren't rationally linked. For example, someone who grew up with an alcoholic father who became angry when intoxicated might believe that alcohol makes people angry. Sure, it can for some, but does it always? There are lots of people who drink alcohol and do not get angry when intoxicated. Here, alcohol becomes a perceived threat. For Jeffery, the gas station became a perceived threat.

When faced with a normally innocuous trigger that has been overcoupled, the body reacts just as it always does to a perceived threat. There is often a tensing of the body, a sense of fear, restricted breathing, and a quick reaction to escape or avoid the triggering stimulus. Once again, you go into that fight, flight, or freeze mode. Overcoupling can create a variety of arousal symptoms, such as anxiety, panic attacks, and severe avoidance, to name a few. Working through overcoupling is a process that's best completed with a licensed therapist. However, you can learn some healthy coping skills to help you feel safer in your environment on a regular basis. Remember, the fact that you experienced danger in a situation before doesn't mean that it will happen again.

Feeling Safer

Now that you have a greater understanding of overcoupling, let's complete a three-step exercise to help you feel safer anywhere you go. Guided visualization can help you feel calmer in situations in which you may feel unsafe, anxious, or overwhelmed. Begin by finding a quiet, relaxing place to sit that feels comfortable to you.

Step 1: Think about a time and place when you felt safe, and answer the following questions.

Where are you?

_____

_____

As you look around you in this memory, describe in detail what you see.

_____

_____

_____

Who, if anyone, is there with you?

_____

_____

Why does this space feel safe to you?

_____

_____

How do you know that you feel safe? What changes in your body to alert you that you're feeling safe?

_____

_____

As you think about yourself sitting in this place, use your senses to describe the scene. What do you see, smell, taste, touch, and hear?

_____

_____

Step 2: Now that you've painted a detailed picture of your place, take a moment to practice sitting in this space in your mind. Find somewhere comfortable to sit or lie down. Close your eyes and imagine this scene in as much detail as you possibly can. Try to imagine it as if you're actually there. Be in this space for as long as you need to.

Step 3: Once you come back into the room, take a quick inventory of how you feel. Do you feel safe? Do you feel calmer? Is your body lighter? Are your senses keener? Take a moment to journal about this experience.

_____

_____

_____

_____

_____

_____

_____

What Have You Learned?

Now that you've completed chapter 6, let's take a moment to think about what you learned. Use the space provided to journal your thoughts about what knowledge you gained here and what changes you'd like to make to improve your life. You may like to use the following questions to get started: How would you like to change the way you talk to yourself? What past situations do you find yourself ruminating on and how might you deal with this moving forward? What changes in your behavior have you noticed after leaving the abusive relationship? How will you navigate these changes in behavior moving forward?

_____

_____

_____

_____

_____

_____

_____

QUICK TIPS AND STRATEGIES TO HANDLE NEGATIVE THINKING

Negative thinking can bring down your mood and negatively impact your outlook on life. Additionally, constant negative thinking can lower your immune system and foster continual stress. If you find yourself having negative thoughts often, you can contain them with these quick tips. Don't get discouraged if this feels hard at first—with practice, it will get easier.

- Use reframing to turn your negative thoughts into positive ones.
- When you catch yourself getting stuck in negative thoughts, think of a happy memory instead.
- Instead of ruminating on something that went wrong, ask yourself, "What can I learn from this?"
- Mentally tell yourself that you're ready to let this negative thought go, and imagine it floating away on a cloud or in a bubble.
- Switch mental gears and focus on your strengths.

CHAPTER TAKEAWAYS

- Talking negatively to yourself can adversely impact your overall well-being. Remember to treat yourself with the same kindness you would for others, and reframe negative self-talk into more positive words for yourself.
- Replacing *should* with *could* can decrease feelings of guilt and shame. If you find that you are should-ing yourself, take a moment to reframe the sentence to be less self-shaming.
- Ruminating on the past is often unhelpful and can facilitate negative thinking. Remember to stay focused in the present so you can move forward on your journey of healing and empowerment.
- Feeling unsafe in an environment is common for survivors of domestic violence. Recognizing your safety-seeking behaviors and working on coping can give you the power to feel safer in your environment.
- Negative thinking can be bad for your health and your well-being. Combat negative thinking to reshape your thoughts into more positive, healthy ones.

healthy communication

Tom's Story

Tom decided to seek therapy after an emotionally abusive relationship with his former partner, Giselle. Upon meeting, Tom described himself as "conflict avoidant" and noted a desire to be able to communicate more effectively to get his own needs met. Tom was ashamed to talk about the abuse to anyone because he felt like no one would believe him.

When they were together, Giselle would become enraged whenever Tom tried to stand up for himself. After years of this, he eventually learned that saying no to Giselle would start a huge conflict, so he learned it was just easier to say yes to anything she wanted to do. Her needs became his needs, and over time, he felt like he wasn't even sure what he wanted for himself anymore.

After the relationship ended, he attempted to confide in his sister, who he thought would understand. Instead of being supportive, she called him silly and told him that he needed to just "be a man and suck it up and get over it." This increased the feeling of shame Tom felt about the relationship, and he decided it was best to keep the abuse secret. For many years, Tom suffered in shame and silence because he felt like a failure as a man for allowing someone to abuse him the way Giselle did. Through therapy, Tom was able to learn that the abuse was not his fault and that a disagreement doesn't always dissolve into a huge conflict.

COMMUNICATING EFFECTIVELY

Communication is an interactive process of both sending and receiving messages between two or more people. This may sound easy, but many people struggle with effective communication. Often, when we think of what communication is, the spoken word generally comes to mind as the central concept; however, there's more to communication than just speaking. You can think of it like a puzzle: The brain must quickly analyze several parts to piece together the meaning of a verbal message. The following are all aspects of communication that we evaluate:

- Words
- Intonation
- Facial expressions
- Body language
- Listener's reactions

As humans, we subconsciously use all of these cues to pick up on the intended meaning of someone's message. Each piece of communication can drastically change the meaning of a message, based on subtle differences. For instance, raising your tone slightly (intonation) at the end of a sentence sends a message that you are asking a question. Keeping your tone level would indicate a statement. Similarly, smiling while talking with someone would indicate a lighthearted, friendly conversation, whereas one during which someone is frowning while talking would indicate that they're angry or upset. If you're mindful of all the aspects of communication, your message has a greater likelihood of being heard and read by the recipient in the way you intended.

Increasing Effective Communication

For this exercise, you'll need an electronic device that can play online videos. You might use a search engine to find free videos on the web. Find a video online that you've never seen before. For example, you could search for clips of an old classic movie or TV show. (Remember to choose something you've never seen before.) Find a comfortable space to sit down, and watch 5 to 10 minutes of this video without sound. (To get the most out of this exercise, it's important to keep the video silent.) Then use this silent video to answer the following questions.

1. **What messages are the characters attempting to convey in this video?**

_____

_____

_____

_____

_____

_____

2. **What emotions are the speakers portraying during this clip?**

_____

_____

_____

_____

_____

3. **Invent a story line for what you're seeing in this clip.**

_____

_____

_____

_____

_____

4. **Now watch the clip again, but this time, turn on the sound.** What messages did you guess correctly just by watching the body language and facial expressions of the actors? What messages did you miss without the words present?

_____

_____

_____

_____

_____

_____

CULTURAL NUANCES OF COMMUNICATION

Believe it or not, communication standards are not universal across all people. Culture plays a large role in how we learn to communicate, with two main types of communication: low-context communication and high-context communication.

Low-Context Communication—Cultures that adopt low-context communication take words at face value and use few, if any, context clues to interpret the sender's message. In this communication style, words hold more weight than anything else in the communication. Clarity and directness are factors in cultures with low-context communication.

High-Context Communication—Cultures that adopt high-context communication place much less emphasis on the actual words being spoken and utilize context clues, such as tone and body language, to assess the meaning of what is being said. This is essentially reading between the lines, so to speak. Communication of this sort looks for meaning in what is _not_ said versus what is actually said.

So how do you know which type of communication style you engage in? Your predominant ethnicity (i.e., the cultural values your family most adopts) will generally impact which type of communication style you use most. Where you live will also influence your communication style, and at times, these two cultural communication styles might conflict. This is significant in the United States, where there is a mixture of ethnicities from all over the world. So, you might live in the United States, which has a predominately low-context culture, but your family emigrated from Japan, which has a high-context culture. In this case, you likely have a mixture of both communication styles. The following is a list of selected ethnicities based on communication style in ascending order from low to high context:

- German
- Scandinavian
- American
- British
- French
- Italian
- Spanish
- Mexican
- Greek
- Arab
- African
- Chinese

"My Culture and Communication"

Developing a greater understanding of the inherent cultural nuances that exist can help you communicate more effectively with others. Let's take a moment to think about your cultural communication style. For each statement, place a check mark in the box that best expresses your experience.

Statement	Always or almost always	Sometimes	Never or almost never
I feel more comfortable in communal spaces.			
My identity involves being part of a large group of people.			
My family tends to build relationships slowly with others.			

I prefer to complete projects with a group of people instead of individually.			
When communicating, I use subtle gestures instead of words to communicate what I am saying.			
I look for a hidden meaning in what someone tells me.			
My relationships tend to take time to form and are long-lasting.			
When disagreements happen, it feels personal to me.			
Privacy isn't important to me.			
I view time as flexible. I'll get there when I get there.			
Add the check marks in each column and enter the totals:			

The column with the most check marks corresponds to your type of contextual communication.

Column 1 = High-Context Communication

Column 2 = Mixed High-/Low-Context Communication

Column 3 = Low-Context Communication

NAVIGATING CONFLICT

For many survivors of domestic violence, conflict feels like a frightening event, just as it did for Tom. If you lived in a situation where conflict was constant, it makes sense, now that it's over, that you want nothing to do with it. Unfortunately, we can't avoid every conflict in life, and sometimes the avoidance of conflict exacerbates the problem. Luckily, there are techniques for navigating conflict you can use that will result in compassion and understanding instead of fighting.

Developed by psychologist Dr. Marshall Rosenberg, nonviolent communication techniques are the gold standard for effective, kind communication that results in peaceful conflict resolution. By using these techniques, you can manage conflict with ease and arrive at resolutions that everyone will feel good about. Sounds easy, right? Well, it's much easier said than done. Let's look at the central tenets of nonviolent communication you can practice when conflict arises. Always remember, conflict is about finding a solution to a problem, not about winning or losing.

Observation—When we communicate with others, observation is about noticing what is happening, without judgment. The action in this step is to communicate what you are hearing and observing to the other person in a neutral manner. For instance, you might say, "I hear you saying . . ." or "What I understand is that . . . ." By paraphrasing back, in a neutral tone, what the person is saying, you're letting them know you are listening and care about what they're saying.

Feeling—When we deal with conflict, our emotions can sometimes take over, and this increases the conflict. The goal here is to separate your feelings from your thoughts so you can continue to communicate in a neutral tone. It's okay to say how you're feeling during a conflict, but sometimes these feelings can lead to blaming others instead of just stating how you feel. Here's an example:

"You never do the laundry."
versus
"I'm feeling resentful because it seems as if I'm doing a lot of the laundry."

Needs—Everyone has needs, and a great deal of conflict resolution means acknowledging others' needs, stating your own needs, and finding a way to get everyone's needs met. Of course, there are times when everyone's needs may not be able to be met, so compromise is necessary. In this way, each person can have some of their needs met. This results in greater equality within the exchange.

Request—Effective communication involves being able to state what your needs are and ask for what you need. This goal goes hand in hand with needs, described in the previous section. Sometimes, when we're communicating, we think that others ought to just know something. The truth is they may not know what your needs are, so it is up to you to state them clearly and neutrally. This is an essential part of clear and direct communication. This is also about cooperation within the communication. A request may be to ask someone if they're willing to hear your needs and cooperate to see if they might be met somehow.

Practicing Compassionate Communication

Let's put some of these nonviolent communication goals into practice. For each statement, rephrase the sentence to be more compassionate, using the four nonviolent communication actions of observation, feeling, needs, and request. There are hints after each sentence to help you know which form of nonviolent communication to use.

Example: "Why did you let the dog run into the house all muddy?"
(Needs and Request)

In the future, could you please remember to wipe the dog's paws when he comes in the house? It helps me keep our house clean.

1. **"You always take me for granted."** (Feeling)

2. **"You're never there for me when I need you."** (Feeling)

3. **"I'm having a hard day and just need some time to myself."** (Observation)

4. "Today was so frustrating! I got a flat tire, my boss said my project at work wasn't good enough, and my rent check bounced." (Observation)

_____

_____

_____

5. "Why can't you just leave me alone?" (Needs)

_____

_____

_____

6. "You never call me anymore! You must not care about me." (Needs)

_____

_____

_____

7. "It's fine! I'll just do everything myself." (Request)

_____

_____

_____

8. "I'm trying to talk to you! Why do you keep ignoring me and looking at your phone?" (Request)

_____

_____

_____

"YOU SHOULD BE OVER THAT BY NOW"

If survivors had a dime for every time they heard some well-intentioned person tell them to "just get over the abuse and move on," they'd be rich. Unfortunately, statements like these lead to more guilt and shame, which you're already trying to get rid of. Sadly, Tom's story about his sister's unsupportive response is all too common. As we talked about in chapter 6, the word *should* is guilt inducing and suggests you're doing something wrong.

There is no formula for how long it takes to heal and move forward from your abusive relationship. For some, it can take decades to feel whole again, and for others, it might take only a couple of months. Statements like "Just get over it and move on" are more about the other person than you. People will sometimes brush off others' pain to avoid their own discomfort with the subject. Also, these statements are bad advice. Healing means taking the time to process what happened and heal, not avoiding the feelings so you can speed ahead like nothing happened.

How to handle this type of statement effectively will depend on how much you value the person saying it. If you don't know the person well, you might choose to ignore the statement and make a mental note that they aren't one of those supportive people in your life. Conversely, if it's someone you're close to, you may find it helpful to educate them on your healing process and let them know that there's no timeline for healing in these scenarios.

This is also a chance to use effective communication skills already discussed in this chapter to let the person know how this type of statement lands with you. For instance, you might respond with something along the lines of "I'm working on my healing process, and I'm wondering, would you be willing to support me by listening with less judgment?" Either way, remind yourself that you are doing the best that you can, and it's okay to take all the time you need to process and move forward.

"I'm Not Over It and That's Okay"

Take a moment to think about a time when someone told you, "You should be over that by now" or something very similar. We can't change what's already happened, but we can think about how we might respond differently in the future. Using the following questions, journal about how you'd like to handle these types of situations when they come up in the future. What did this person say to you? What was your response when it happened?

What would you like to do differently next time? How might you use the effective communication skills discussed in this chapter to respond to similar statements?

_____

_____

_____

_____

_____

_____

_____

_____

_____

_____

_____

_____

Silence as a Weapon

Have you ever heard the phrase, "If you don't have anything nice to say, don't say anything at all"? In our society, silence is often seen as taking the high road to decrease conflict. Truthfully, silence can actually be a passive-aggressive behavior that throws gasoline on the fire. You may have experienced silence as a form of abuse in your relationship. Abusers will refuse to talk any longer and will walk away from the argument with the air of "I'm too good for this conflict." Or they may have used silence to ignore your presence in the room.

There's a difference between not saying something to avoid hurting some-one's feelings and giving someone silence as an act of aggression. If you're the type of person who uses silence when you're angry or upset, think about how this may impact the conflict and the other person. You may be increasing the conflict without realizing it. Not speaking to someone for an extended period of time is one example of using silence as a weapon, because the other person knows that you are upset with them. There can be no resolution without com-munication. Using silence only prolongs the conflict and creates further upset.

The next time you have the urge to give someone the silent treatment, think about how this might hinder a timely resolution.

THE IMPORTANCE OF SAYING NO (EVEN WHEN YOU'VE ALREADY SAID YES)

In chapter 2, we talked about assertiveness and the importance of getting your needs met. Being able to say no when you want to is an effective assertiveness skill and also a good communication skill. After experiencing an abusive relationship, you may feel nervous about saying no to someone, just as Tom experienced. This is totally normal. When your power has been taken away, often your ability to comfortably say no is also gone. It's okay to say no when you want to, even when you already said yes. It may take practice to once again feel comfortable saying no, and that's okay. Being able to say no can increase your sense of empowerment because you are advocating for your own well-being.

Have you ever said yes, only to wish moments later that you'd said no? Sometimes we say yes to something because we don't take the time to think it through before respond-ing. There may be fear that if you say no, there will be conflict or that it might damage a valued relationship. You always have the option of asking for time to consider someone's request so you can think it over and make the decision you're most comfortable with.

When saying no to someone, use your new superpower of assertiveness to calmly say no and be clear about your message. Making excuses or waffling with your response may send the message that you're unsure about your response. This can lead to others pushing your boundaries, making saying no even harder. If someone does push your boundaries, stand firm in your no. It's alright to stand up for your own needs. Saying yes to everything will leave you with no time to get your own needs met. Additionally, saying no helps you live your life more authentically, which can lead to a happier life.

Saying No Like You Mean It

Take a moment to think about a time recently when you said yes to someone but you really wish you had said no. Let's spend some time journaling about how you might change that yes to a no or how you might navigate this situation more effectively in the future. You could address some or all of the following questions: What were the circumstances surrounding the situation you said yes to? What stopped you from saying no? What fears come up when you think about saying no to this situation? Would you have made a different decision if you asked for some time to think about it instead of answering right away? What do you think might have happened if you decided to say no instead of yes? Is that possible now? If not, what might you do differently in the future to say no instead of yes?

_____

_____

_____

_____

_____

_____

_____

_____

_____

_____

_____

_____

COMMUNICATING WITH A FORMER ABUSER

The rule of thumb for communicating with a former abuser is simple: Don't! It's best for you to cease all contact with your former abuser as soon as possible. There may be times when you feel tempted to reach out to your abuser because you miss that person. Unfortunately, caving in can create setbacks for your healing process. Continued communication with an abuser can lead to more emotional abuse through manipulation, so it's always best to put that relationship in the past.

Abusers will often use any means they can to continue to assert power and control, even long after you've left the relationship. Ceasing communication may mean blocking their number in your cellphone, deleting connections on social media, deleting the abuser's associates from your social media, and refusing to answer their emails. In extreme cases, it may even mean relocating. Ceasing communication may feel hard at times, but it's the healthiest option for you to be able to move forward.

Unfortunately, there are many situations in which it's not possible to cease all communication with a former abuser. Ongoing legal proceedings, shared childcare, asset division, and postdivorce financial arrangements are all examples of situations where some communication with your abuser might be inevitable. Abusers will use all of these scenarios to continue to abuse if they're given the chance. While still in an abusive relationship, survivors often wonder how they can communicate more effectively with their abusive partner. In a healthy relationship, that goal could absolutely be possible. In the context of an abusive relationship, it's often not possible because the abuser isn't interested in healthy communication—they are interested only in maintaining power and control. If you find yourself having to communicate with an abusive ex-partner, here are some helpful tips to maintain your power:

- Approach conversations as a business transaction.
- Set aside your emotions.
- Talk in a calm, neutral tone.
- Don't get roped in to discussing issues from the past.
- Say no when you need to.
- Be assertive.
- Use electronic communication so you have a record of what is said.
- Stick to the facts and stand your ground.
- Use a court-monitored online communication application for highly conflictual situations.
- Ask your lawyer to relay messages if you have one.
- Ask law enforcement to accompany you to collect your assets.
- Walk away from the conversation if it starts to feel abusive.

Staying Strong

After an abusive relationship ends, it can be hard to cut off all communication. As mentioned earlier, feelings of loneliness and isolation can tempt you to contact your ex-partner. Although you may feel short-term relief by reaching out, the long-term effects are not worth it. The key to staying strong and not communicating with your ex-partner is to find healthier ways to get your needs met. The good news is that the temptation to contact your ex-partner will fade over time. Until then, take a look at the following and see what healthier alternatives you may have.

1. **When you have thoughts about contacting your ex, who are two other safe, supportive people you could call?** If you feel like you don't have anyone safe to call yet, write down a crisis support line to call. You don't need to be in crisis to talk with one of their counselors. You can call just to talk with someone if that's all you need. (You'll find crisis lines in the Resources section on page 131.)

_____

_____

_____

_____

2. **List two activities you could do instead of contacting your ex.** Some examples are going for a walk, heading to the gym, or creating art.

_____

_____

_____

_____

3. **List two places you could go to get your mind off your ex.** For instance, there may be a park close by that you enjoy walking through, or you could head to the library (where phones are frowned on).

_____

_____

4. **Think of three reasons why it wouldn't be a good idea to contact your abusive ex-partner and write them down here.** When you have the urge to contact this person, remind yourself of these three powerful reasons to stay strong.

_____

_____

_____

_____

5. **Make a list of the gains you've made since leaving your abusive relationship.** When you have the urge to contact this person, remind yourself of these awesome reasons to stay strong.

_____

_____

_____

_____

What Have You Learned?

Now that you've completed chapter 7, let's think about what you learned. Use the space provided to journal your thoughts about what knowledge you gained here and what changes you'd like to make to improve your life. You could answer some or all of the following questions: What new communication skills do you think will be most helpful for you? How will you practice these skills and incorporate them into your life? How can you say no when you want to? How does your culture contribute to your communication style? Are there ways to decrease or eliminate communication with an abusive ex-partner?

_____

_____

_____

_____

_____

_____

_____

_____

_____

_____

_____

_____

_____

_____

QUICK TIPS AND STRATEGIES FOR COMPASSIONATE COMMUNICATION

Choosing words carefully can also go a long way toward effective communication. Even when we mean well, we can choose words that automatically place someone on the defensive, which creates unintentional conflict. Here are some helpful tips to communicate in a way that will increase your chances of having your message interpreted as helpful instead of hurtful:

- Use "I" statements instead of "you" statements.
- Avoid extreme qualifiers, such as "always" or "never."
- Be direct and clear about what you are saying.
- Try to not jump to conclusions. Ask clarifying questions instead.
- Wait until your emotions settle before approaching the conversation if you feel emotional about something you need to discuss.
- Don't assume what someone means by something. Ask clarifying questions to make sure you understand the message being conveyed.
- Have important conversations face-to-face. Electronic communication lacks many important communication cues we rely on to interpret messages.

CHAPTER TAKEAWAYS

- Effective communication involves evaluating words as well as more subtle nuances, such as body language, intonation, and facial expression. To get our message across as intended, we need to be mindful of not only what we say but also how we say it.

- Culture plays a large role in the style of communication we use. Depending on your culture, you may place more or less emphasis on what is actually said.

- Avoiding conflict may exacerbate relationship disagreements. Using nonviolent communication skills can help turn conflict into mutual problem solving.

- Recovering from an abusive relationship does not have any expected timeline. You can take all the time you need to heal.

- Learning how to say no can help you feel more empowered and allow you to live your life more authentically.

- Communication with a former abuser is not advised, but if you must, try to remain calm and use your support system as much as you need to.

moving on to healthy relationships

Maya's Story

Maya is a 42-year-old woman who ended her abusive relationship after 23 years of marriage. When the relationship ended, she had no interest in dating. In fact, she felt fearful of ever dating again. After enduring so much abuse, she experienced difficulty trusting anyone outside of her family and decided that she would rather focus on her career and adult children instead of a relationship. Sure, Maya had some family nearby who were supportive during her divorce; however, she felt lonely at times with no real friends to support her. The "old" Maya loved going out and socializing and never had any issues making friends. While she was married, her husband did not allow her to leave the house unattended and forbade her from hanging out with her friends, saying they were "trashy and worthless." Three years after the divorce, Maya met a man at the bookstore who flirted with her and gave her his number. Maya thought he was kind and attractive, but she still felt hesitant to call him for a date. She worried that he might be abusive, just like her ex-husband. Deep down she knew she never wanted to experience that kind of relationship again and held little hope that she could have a healthy relationship in the future. Still, she felt lonely and wanted to have someone to share her life with, so she decided to give him a call.

SIGNS OF A HEALTHY RELATIONSHIP

Maya's story of fear and difficulty trusting strangers is all too common after an abusive relationship. After experiencing abuse, it can seem scary to think about dating again; however, it is possible to have a healthy relationship in the future. So what exactly is a healthy relationship, and how do you know if you're in one? Well, as we've discussed throughout this book, abusive relationships involve skewed power dynamics. So equality is the logical answer to what makes a relationship healthy. Equality will look different for everyone and will depend on each person's needs in the relationship; however, there are some basic tenets of equality in relationships. In the next section, we'll talk about red flags that can indicate skewed power dynamics so you can watch for them. For now, let's talk about equality and what that looks like.

Relationship equality involves give-and-take on the part of both partners. This means that there's shared power and equal decision making. The basic tenets of a healthy relationship are mutual respect, consent, trust, open communication, safety, and nonviolence. Let's take a look at each of these more closely.

Mutual Respect—Mutual respect in a relationship means that each person values the other. This involves respecting boundaries, listening to the other's opinions, responding to each partner's needs, being open to alternative views, and sometimes agreeing to disagree. Mutual respect is about respecting another person as an autonomous human being and valuing their thoughts, goals, and achievements.

Consent—Consent involves each person agreeing to the terms of the relationship. The word *consent* is often defined as bodily consent and certainly applies here; however, there's more than that to consent in a relationship. Consent involves mutual agreements about dynamics in the relationship. With consent, power can be shifted in a healthy way. For instance, if two people in a relationship agree that one will handle the finances and the other will cook and clean, then each partner has consented to their share of power in the relationship. Lack of consent happens when one person demands to have the power in some or all aspects of the relationship. This happens when, for example, one partner manages all the finances and does not allow the other partner to access financial resources.

Trust—Trust is a cornerstone of all healthy relationships and involves complete honesty on the part of both partners. When there is trust, jealousy is decreased because each person knows that the other is being honest. When trust is established, each partner is able to spend time both together and separately without issue. To facilitate trust, partners need to believe in what the other says.

Open Communication—Open communication involves being completely honest and open to discussing anything in the relationship. To have open communication, partners need to react well to difficult conversations, and each partner creates a safe space to discuss any topic. This often requires both partners to sit in the uncomfortable space of vulnerability with each other.

Nonviolence—Nonviolence in a relationship means that partners are emotionally supportive and do not engage in physical violence, manipulation, threats, or coercion.

Safety—Safety involves not only feeling physically safe with your partner but also feeling safe from emotional harm. Safety can be fostered through open communication, trust, nonviolence, mutual respect, and consent. When safety is established, you are sure in the knowledge that your partner has your best interests at heart and would never do anything to intentionally harm you.

Relationship Role Models

Sometimes having role models for healthy relationships can help us gain a greater understanding of what kind of relationship we would like to have moving forward. For this exercise, think about the people you know and identify people you think have a healthy relationship. Of course, having a healthy relationship doesn't mean that they never have problems; but if they're able to come together during their difficulties to work things out in a healthy way, that is really what matters.

Who is someone in your life who attempts to incorporate mutual respect, consent, trust, open communication, nonviolence, and safety? If you can't think of just one person who embodies all of these relationship values, you can use several people you know to complete this exercise. For instance, maybe you have a friend who uses honesty effectively to create trust and a family member who does a great job of setting and respecting boundaries with their partner.

Relationship value	Role model	How does this person achieve this value?
Mutual respect		
Consent		
Trust		
Open communication		
Nonviolence		
Safety		

RELATIONSHIP RED FLAGS

Red flags are the warning signs that are important to pay attention to as they come up in a new relationship. Most often, these show up as feelings of uneasiness or the sense that something just doesn't feel right to you. Most survivors of domestic violence say there were red flags early on in the abusive relationship, but they either rationalized them away or ignored them. Listen to your gut! These red flags are worth paying attention to so your next relationship is a healthy one.

In chapter 1, we outlined different types of abusive relationships, and you completed an exercise to assess the types of abuse you survived (Identifying Acts of Domestic Violence, page 4). All of the examples listed in that exercise are red flags that your relationship may be wandering into abusive territory. When considering a new relationship, it would be worthwhile to review that list and watch out for any of those abusive behaviors in your new relationship. If you notice something that feels like a red flag in a new relationship, use your new superpowers of assertiveness and healthy communication to discuss your concerns with your partner.

If your partner is unwilling to discuss these with you and refuses to take accountability, these are two huge red flags that this is not likely be a healthy relationship. The following is a list of common red flags that indicate an unhealthy relationship is on the horizon. Obviously, physical abuse is a huge red flag; however, most abuse starts with emotional abuse, so the warning signs on the list are usually present prior to the physical abuse.

- Refusing to take accountability (i.e., blaming others for everything that goes wrong)
- Showing difficulty with vulnerability
- Acting like they are always right and you are always wrong
- Exhibiting jealous behaviors, even about spending time with friends and family
- Displaying a "my way or the highway" kind of attitude
- Wanting commitment very early on in the relationship
- Violating your privacy, such as reading your emails or listening to your phone calls
- Demanding to know where you are at all times
- Installing tracking on your electronic devices
- Telling you what to wear or who you can spend time with
- Belittling you, calling you names, or laughing at you
- Telling you that your emotions are silly or not valid
- Giving you ultimatums
- Lacking empathy
- Lying and/or cheating
- Showering you with lavish gifts, attention, and affection early on in the relationship
- Refusing to compromise
- Demanding sex, pressuring you for sex, or asking you to perform sexual acts that you have already said you're uncomfortable with
- Pushing your boundaries and refusing to take no for an answer
- Becoming verbally aggressive when you attempt to stand up for yourself
- Requesting to control your finances or telling you what kinds of jobs you can have

"My Red Flags"

Back in chapter 2, you created a list of red flags that you overlooked in your previous relationship (Watching Out for Controlling Behavior, page 31). Let's take a moment to review that list of red flags again. Next to each number, write a red flag from your list in the chapter 2 exercise and circle the relationship values that were being violated by that behavior. This will help you have a greater understanding of exactly why these red flags were unhealthy in your relationship and what to look out for in the future.

1. **red flag: mutual respect consent trust open communication nonviolence safety**
2. **red flag: mutual respect consent trust open communication nonviolence safety**
3. **red flag: mutual respect consent trust open communication nonviolence safety**
4. **red flag: mutual respect consent trust open communication nonviolence safety**
5. **red flag: mutual respect consent trust open communication nonviolence safety**
6. **red flag: mutual respect consent trust open communication nonviolence safety**
7. **red flag: mutual respect consent trust open communication nonviolence safety**
8. **red flag: mutual respect consent trust open communication nonviolence safety**
9. **red flag: mutual respect consent trust open communication nonviolence safety**
10. **red flag: mutual respect consent trust open communication nonviolence safety**

DEVELOPING POSITIVE CONNECTIONS

Healing from domestic violence requires developing positive connections with other, supportive people. When social isolation has occurred as a result of an abusive relationship, it can feel daunting to start from scratch and find friends. Creating a new social circle takes time and dedication, but it's well worth the work. In fact, creating supportive platonic relationships is a lot like dating.

Developing healthy relationships is a gradual process of getting to know someone so that trust can develop between the two of you. When you first meet someone who could be a potential friend, there's a courtship of sorts that takes place as you each assess if the other person is an acquaintance or a long-term friend. Often, this stage is superficial in nature, and it's important to have healthy boundaries around what you share with them. For instance, you wouldn't want to tell someone all of your problems the first time you meet.

You may hang out a few times to see if you have things in common, and as you gradually start to trust them, you can start to talk with them more openly about your life. It's a good idea to start small to see how they handle it when you discuss difficult things in your life. When you do, a supportive friend is someone who will listen, have empathy for you, and provide the type of support you need in that moment. Just like it is in romantic relationships, trust is a cornerstone of a healthy, supportive friendship.

So, how exactly do you meet new potential friends? It's hard, especially as an adult! If you're unsure where to start to create a new social circle, here are a few ideas for places to meet people with interests similar to yours. This is also a great way to develop more hobbies, which provide coping skills and self-care!

- Start conversations with coworkers or invite a coworker to have coffee/tea.
- Join a social meetup group.
- Join a sports activity group or book club.
- Ask an acquaintance to teach you something you've always wanted to learn (e.g., knitting or welding).
- Take a class at your community center.
- Start a group for an interest you have (e.g., playing board games).
- Take your dog to the dog park and strike up conversations with other dog owners.
- Schedule kid playdates with other parents in your neighborhood.
- Go to events in your community.
- Volunteer at a local nonprofit.
- Organize a potluck lunch and ask friends to invite other friends.
- Visit your local public library and check for free and low-cost activities.

The Friend Zone

Increasing social engagement can feel overwhelming at first. Let's take a moment to explore how you might meet new people so you can have a road map to new, healthy relationships. Think about each of the following questions and write your answers on the lines provided. Look online to find some answers to these questions if you feel stumped.

1. **What hobbies do you already have or would like to start up again?**

_____

_____

2. **What activities or hobbies have you thought about trying?**

_____

_____

3. What groups already exist in your area for the hobbies or activities you'd like to engage in?

_____

_____

4. **Who are the acquaintances in your life you think could make good long-term friends?** (All it takes is one person to get the ball rolling.)

_____

_____

5. What activities or events might you ask these acquaintances to attend with you to spark a friendship?

_____

_____

6. What classes would you be interested in taking?

_____

_____

7. If you were to volunteer for a nonprofit, what types of philanthropic causes do you feel compelled to support?

_____

_____

8. If you listed nonprofit causes you would like to support, what are the organizations in your area that could provide volunteer opportunities for these?

_____

_____

Creating Your Phenomenal Team

Having friends and family for different support needs in your life can help fill gaps in your social support needs. One friend may be great at listening to you vent when you've had a rough day at work, whereas another friend might have the capacity to be available for support on a moment's notice. Or a certain family member may have a knack for making you smile when you're feeling down. Having good friends doesn't mean that each person has to fulfill all your support needs. Thinking about the strengths each person offers, and utilizing those strengths when you need support, can help you create a phenomenal team of care for different difficulties in your life.

Knowing who to call and when not only increases the quality of your support network but also can decrease disappointment in relationships. Calling on the people in your support group who are the best fit for your needs in that moment decreases the chances that you'll feel let down by someone. For instance, if you have a friend with seven children, that person may not have the capacity to drive you to the doctor on short notice because of their hectic parenting schedule. If you were to ask this person for last-minute support, you might feel unsupported when they say no, even though it's not personal. Remember to be realistic about who you lean on for what types of support so you can increase your chances of feeling supported by the people who care about you.

CHANGING UNHEALTHY RELATIONSHIPS

While reading this section on healthy relationships, you may have started thinking more analytically about your relationships with friends, coworkers, and family. Sometimes, these types of relationships can be unhealthy, too. If you've noticed unhealthy patterns in platonic relationships that you value, you have the power to advocate for healthier ways of relating with each other. Additionally, relationships with loved ones can become strained as a result of an abusive relationship. It may take some time to repair the relationship, but with some dedication and patience, relationships you thought were lost can often be repaired.

In chapter 7, we discussed healthy communication. Being able to communicate your feelings is a central tenet of healthy relationships and the perfect place to start improving any unhealthy relationships you may have. Additionally, being open and honest is also an important factor that helps facilitate change. Changing unhealthy relationships is a collaborative process that can be rewarding over the long term. Here are some helpful tips to advocate for better, healthier relationships with your loved ones:

- Tell them how much you value them in your life.
- Let them know that you'd like to work on improving your relationship.
- Ask if they would be willing to talk about how to improve the relationship.
- Discuss your feelings openly about what feels like it's not working well.
- Identify some shared goals moving forward to help strengthen the relationship.
- Avoid statements that blame the other for the difficulties in the relationship.
- Tell them honestly what you need from the relationship.
- Express what you feel is missing from the relationship.
- Tell them what you appreciate about them.
- Be open to feedback about how you may be contributing to difficulties in the relationship.
- Acknowledge your shortcomings in the relationship.
- Validate their feelings.
- Identify ways you can be a better friend, coworker, or family member.

Patching Up Relationships

If you have someone in your life you'd like to improve your relationship with, take a moment to think about the following questions. Then journal about how you would start a conversation with them. If you get stuck, look back at the tips provided in the previous section on how to advocate for healthier relationships. Who do you think would be open to such a discussion? How would you start the conversation? How do you currently feel about the relationship? What do you feel is working in the relationship? What improvements do you think would be helpful? How can the two of you collaborate together to make some changes toward these improvements? What do you value about this relationship, and why is it so important to you?

_____

_____

_____

_____

_____

_____

_____

_____

_____

_____

_____

_____

_____

_____

TALKING ABOUT RECOVERY TO FRIENDS AND FAMILY

In chapter 3, we talked about breaking the silence regarding abuse, and this can also help foster meaningful relationships. Many survivors are surprised to hear that other people they know have experienced something similar, which can be part of the healing process. Opening up to others requires vulnerability, which can often be hard after experiencing abuse. There are many benefits to talking with friends and family about your recovery, such as increased social support, assistance with accountability for change, strengthened connections, increased awareness for your struggles, and decreasing stigma. Not everyone will be supportive, so it's important to gauge emotional safety before you discuss your traumatic experience with others. A person who is unsupportive can create more emotional harm, so think analytically about who you want to talk to about your experience and healing process.

Talking with friends and family doesn't mean you have to disclose all the details of your abusive relationship or healing process. It is always up to you how much you disclose and what you feel safe discussing with each person.

Opening Up

Take a moment to think about who might be supportive for you to talk with about your healing process and how you might facilitate this. Think about the following questions and write your answers in the spaces provided.

1. **Which one or two people you know feel the safest to start talking with about your healing process?**

_____

_____

2. **What is it about this person or people that makes you think that they would be supportive?**

_____

_____

3. **What benefits do you anticipate from sharing your story with them?**

_____

_____

4. **Which parts of your story feel the scariest to share with these people?**

_____

_____

5. **Which parts of your story feel the safest to share with these people?**

_____

_____

6. **How would you like to be supported in your healing process by these people?**

_____

_____

FUTURE PARTNERS

With each relationship that hasn't worked, you have learned more about what you do and do not want in a partner. This is valuable information as you move forward in the Wild West of the dating world! It's important to note that there's no fixed formula, and it's your personal choice when to start dating again. What I can say is that it's important to heal from your previous relationship before moving on to the next one. When we don't allow ourselves enough time to heal, we can unconsciously bring baggage into the new relationship, which complicates things. Sometimes survivors jump from one relationship into another, which often turns out to be disastrous for many reasons. Taking things slow means that you take time to assess whether or not a potential partner has the qualities you need in a relationship. Remember, it's okay to take the time you need to get to know your next partner before making a commitment. Don't let someone pressure you into a new relationship before you feel ready.

Your Road Map to a Healthy Relationship

Now that you know how to strengthen your relationships with the supportive people already in your life, let's take a moment to think about what to look for in a future romantic partner. You may not be ready to date just yet, and that's okay. This exercise will help you in the future whenever you're ready. Let's use your previous relationship experiences to make a list of both desirable and undesirable traits for your new partner. You deserve to have someone who treats you well and meets all of your needs in a relationship!

Sit back and imagine your ideal partner. What personality characteristics does this person have? Note these in the "desirable traits" category. Then think about your past relationships: What characteristics did your partner have that didn't work for you? Note those in the "undesirable traits" category. Sometimes, it can be easier to think of the not-so-great characteristics of our previous relationships. If that is the case for you, feel free to complete the "undesirable traits" first and use that as a guide for your "desirable traits" by writing down the opposite of the undesirable ones. Also, it can be helpful to think of your past relationships and note things that you felt were missing from each of them, which can go in your "desirable traits" category.

Once you have finished making this list, go back through the "desirable traits" category and put a star in the first column by the ones that are non-negotiables. Non-negotiables are the traits your next partner *must* have for you to be truly happy. When you consider dating again, refer to this list to make sure your next partner has many, if not all, of the qualities that you desire. And pay special attention to your non-negotiables, which would be considered dealbreakers if the potential partner does not have them.

Non-negotiable	Desirable traits	Undesirable traits

What Have You Learned?

Now that you've completed chapter 8, let's take a moment to think about what you learned. Use the provided space to journal your thoughts about what knowledge you gained here and what changes you'd like to make to improve your life. What signs will you look for in a healthy relationship? What red flags will you watch out for with a future partner? How will you create new relationships and mend old ones? How will you open up to friends and family about your healing process?

QUICK TIPS FOR SAFE DATING

When you decide to date again, remember that safety is always the number one priority! This is true for anyone in the dating world, not only someone who's experienced an abusive relationship. Safety is especially important in the age of online dating because you never know who is actually going to show up to your date. Here are some safety tips when meeting someone new for the first time:

- Meet in a public place.
- Let someone you trust know where you are going and what time you expect to be home.
- Notify your person of trust when you arrive home safely.
- Don't tell your date where you live or where you work.
- Secure your own transportation to and from the date.
- Don't leave your food or drinks unattended.
- Limit alcohol consumption.
- Have an exit plan in place, such as needing to assist a friend.
- Use your assertiveness skills to say no and end the date if it's not going well.

CHAPTER TAKEAWAYS

- It's possible to have a healthy relationship after an abusive one! The key is to understand what a healthy relationship looks like and watch out for red flags.
- Consent, mutual respect, trust, open communication, nonviolence, and safety are the central tenets of a healthy relationship.
- Developing positive connections with safe, supportive people is an important part of the healing process. It takes time to make new friends, and going slow is okay.
- If you notice unhealthy platonic relationships in your life, you can try to turn them around using your effective communication skills.
- Talking to friends and family about your healing process takes guts! It can be a very rewarding process if you take the plunge.
- Learning from your past relationships means you now have a better understanding of what you do and do not want in your next relationship. Use this knowledge to find a partner who fulfills your needs.

RESOURCES

If you're reading this, you've probably completed this workbook, and congratulations are definitely in order because you accomplished something you set out to do. I know you put a lot of effort into our journey together and, at times, some parts may have felt challenging. But you pushed through to the end. I hope that this book helped you on your path toward healing and recovery. Remember, you can always come back and review sections in this book if you ever feel the need. All of your hard work here can serve as a useful resource to keep you on track to achieving your goals. Additionally, the resources below can be helpful if you're looking for more information to help you through this transition process.

Also, remember this: You are strong, powerful, and wise! I wish you all the success on your path to living a life free from abuse.

Hotlines

Crisis Text Line: Text "home" to 741741

National Domestic Violence Hotline: 1-800-799-7233

Websites

Break the Silence: breakthesilencedv.org

The Center for Nonviolent Communication: cnvc.org

The National Coalition Against Domestic Violence: ncadv.org

National Domestic Violence Hotline: thehotline.org

Books

Bancroft, Lundy. *Why Does He Do That? Inside the Minds of Angry and Controlling Men.* New York: Berkeley, 2003.

Brown, Brené. *Daring Greatly: How the Courage to Be Vulnerable Transforms the Way We Live, Love, Parent, and Lead.* New York: Gotham, 2012.

Brown, Brené. *I Thought It Was Just Me (But It Isn't): Making the Journey from "What Will People Think?" to "I Am Enough."* New York: Avery, 2007.

Brown, Brené. *The Gifts of Imperfection: Let Go of Who You Think You're Supposed to Be and Embrace Who You Are*. Center City, MN: Hazelden Publishing, 2010.

David, Susan. *Emotional Agility: Get Unstuck, Embrace Change, and Thrive in Work and Life*. New York: Avery, 2016.

Evans, Patricia Healy. *The Verbally Abusive Relationship: How to Recognize It and How to Respond*. Avon, MA: Adams Media, 2003.

Levine, Peter. *Waking the Tiger: Healing Trauma: The Innate Capacity to Transform Overwhelming Experiences*. Berkeley, CA: North Atlantic Books, 1997.

van der Kolk, Bessel. *The Body Keeps the Score: Brain, Mind, and Body in the Healing of Trauma*. New York: Viking Press, 2014.

Self-Assessment

Cultural Context Inventory: resilitator.com/images/pdf/CulturalContextInventory_ASRC.pdf

REFERENCES

Anderson, Kim M., Lynette M. Renner, and Fran S. Danis. "Recovery: Resilience and Growth in the Aftermath of Domestic Violence." *Violence Against Women* (January 2013): 1279–99. doi:10.1177/1077801212470543.

Brown, Brené. *Daring Greatly: How the Courage to Be Vulnerable Transforms the Way We Live, Love, Parent, and Lead.* New York: Gotham, 2012.

Calhoun, Lawrence G., and Richard G. Tedeschi. *Posttraumatic Growth in Clinical Practice.* New York: Routledge/Taylor & Francis Group, 2013.

Campbell-Sills, Laura, David R. Forde, and Murray B. Stein. "Demographic and Childhood Environmental Predictors of Resilience in a Community Sample." *Journal of Psychiatric Research*, 43 (2009): 1007–12.

Campbell-Sills, Laura, Sharon L. Cohan, and Murray B. Stein. "Relationship of Resilience to Personality, Coping, and Psychiatric Symptoms in Young Adults." *Behaviour Research and Therapy* 44 (2006): 585–99.

Chida, Yoichi, and Andrew Steptoe. "The Association of Anger and Hostility with Future Coronary Heart Disease: A Meta-analytic Review of Prospective Evidence." *Journal of the American College of Cardiology*, 53 (2009): 936–46.

David, Susan A. *Emotional Agility: Get Unstuck, Embrace Change, and Thrive in Work and Life.* New York: Avery, 2016.

Gilbert, P., J. Pehl, and S. Allan. "The Phenomenology of Shame and Guilt: An Empirical Investigation." *British Journal of Medical Psychology* 67 (March 1994): 23–36.

Gottlieb, Dan. "After Trauma: 'Why Me?'" *HuffPost.* Updated April 4, 2012. https://www.huffpost.com/entry/gratitude_b_1251302.

Halford, W. K., E. Keefer, and S. M. Osgarby. "'How Has the Week Been for You Two?' Relationship Satisfaction and Hindsight Memory Biases in Couples' Reports of Relationship Events." *Cognitive Therapy and Research* 26, no. 6 (2002): 759–73. doi:10.1023/A:1021289400436.

Hall, Edward T. *The Silent Language.* Garden City, NY: Doubleday, 1959.

Herman, Judith L. *Trauma and Recovery: The Aftermath of Violence—From Domestic Abuse to Political Terror.* New York: Basic Books, 1997.

Janoff-Bulman, R. *Shattered Assumptions: Toward a New Psychology of Trauma.* New York: Free Press, 1992.

King, Brian. *The Laughing Cure: Emotional and Physical Healing? A Comedian Reveals Why Laughter Really Is the Best Medicine.* New York: Skyhorse Publishing, 2016.

Krauss Whitborne, Susan. "The Definitive Guide to Guilt: Five Types of Guilt and How You Can Cope with Each." *Psychology Today.* August 11, 2012. https://www.psychologytoday.com/us/blog/fulfillment-any-age/201208/the-definitive-guide-guilt.

Kubany, Edward S., Mari A. McCaig, and Janet R. Laconsay. *Healing the Trauma of Domestic Violence: A Workbook for Women.* Oakland, CA: New Harbinger, 2004.

Levine, Peter. *In an Unspoken Voice: How the Body Releases Trauma and Restores Goodness.* Berkeley, CA: North Atlantic Books, 2010.

Levine, Peter. *Waking the Tiger: Healing Trauma: The Innate Capacity to Transform Overwhelming Experiences.* Berkeley, CA: North Atlantic Books, 1997.

Levine, Stephen Z., Avital Laufer, Einat Stein, Yaira Hamama-Raz, and Zahava Solomon. "Examining the Relationship between Resilience and Posttraumatic Growth." *Journal of Traumatic Stress* 22 (July 2009): 282–86. doi:10.1002/jts.20409.

Masten, Ann S. "Resilience in Individual Development: Successful Adaptation Despite Risk and Adversity." In *Risk and Resilience in Inner City America: Challenges and Prospects*, edited by M. Wang and E. Gordon, 3–26. Hillsdale, NJ: Erlbaum, 1994.

Mendez Ruiz, Ashley. "Self-Defense: An Intervention Technique to Empower Victims of Domestic Violence." Faculty Curated Undergraduate Works, paper 35, Arcadia University, 2016. http://scholarworks.arcadia.edu/undergrad_works/35.

National Coalition Against Domestic Violence. "Domestic Violence and the LGBTQ Community." *NCADV Blog.* June 6, 2018. https://ncadv.org/blog/posts/domestic-violence-and-the-lgbtq-community.

National Domestic Violence Hotline. *Power and Control Wheel, Abuse Defined.* Accessed December 1, 2020. https://www.thehotline.org/is-this-abuse/abuse-defined/power-and-control-wheel-updated.

Rosenberg, Marshall, B. *Nonviolent Communication: A Language of Life*. Encinitas, CA: PuddleDancer Press, 2003.

Simeon, D., R. Yehuda, R. Cunill, M. Knutelska, F. W. Putnam, and L. M. Smith. "Factors Associated with Resilience in Healthy Adults." *Psychoneuroendocrinology* 32, nos. 8–10 (2007): 1149–52. doi:10.1016/j.psyneuen.2007.08.005.

Smith, Manuel J. *When I Say No, I Feel Guilty*. New York: Dial Press, 1985.

Stevenson, Robert Louis. *The Strange Case of Dr. Jekyll and Mr. Hyde*. London: New English Library, 1974.

Tedeschi, Richard G., and Calhoun, Lawrence G. *Trauma and Transformation: Growing in the Aftermath of Suffering*. Thousand Oaks, CA: Sage Publications, 1995.

Tedeschi, Richard G. "Violence Transformed: Posttraumatic Growth in Survivors and Their Societies." *Aggression and Violent Behavior* 4, no. 3 (1999): 319–41. doi:10.1016 /S1359-1789(98)00005-6.

U.S. Department of Justice, Bureau of Justice Statistics, *National Crime Victimization Survey*, Concatenated File, 1992–2015.

van der Kolk, Bessel. *The Body Keeps the Score: Brain, Mind, and Body in the Healing of Trauma*. New York: Viking Press, 2014.

Warshaw, Carole, Cris M. Sullivan, and Echo A. Rivera. *A Systematic Review of Trauma-Focused Interventions for Domestic Violence Survivors*. Chicago: National Center on Domestic Violence, Trauma and Mental Health, 2013. http://www .nationalcenterdvtraumamh.org/wp-content/uploads/2013/03/NCDVTMH _EBPLitReview2013.pdf.

Werdel, M. B., and R. J. Wick. *Primer on Posttraumatic Growth: An Introduction and Guide*. Somerset, NJ: John Wiley & Sons, 2012.

YWCA. *Healthy Relationship Wheel*. Accessed January 10, 2020. https://ywcaspokane.org /wp-content/uploads/2017/10/2018-YWCA-Spokane-Healthy-Relationship-Wheel.pdf.

INDEX

past
  learn from the, 46–48
  relationships, 31, 47,
    127–128, 130
post-traumatic growth (PTG), 15

R

recovery
  explained, 14
  goals of, 16–17
  growth, post-traumatic, 15
  process of, 40, 46, 75, 125
  therapy and, 11
red flags
  recognizing, 21, 23, 30–31
  relationship, 118–119,
    120, 129, 130. *See also*
    behavior, controlling
relationship
  abusive, physical violence, 2–3
  healthy, 23, 27, 31, 110, 115–117,
    119, 123
  improving on, 10, 123–124
  past, 31, 47, 127–128, 130
  platonic, 120, 123, 130
  red flags of, 118–119
  toxic, 53, 56
  unhealthy, 32, 40, 119, 123–124
resilience, 14
resources, 131

response
  anger, as a, 72
  changing your, 64–65
  fear, as to, 20
  guilt and shame,
    feelings of, 38, 39, 40
  negative, as hurtful, 106
  stress, as to, 54, 60

S

safety
  behaviors of, 90–91, 96
  response, as need for, 3, 10,
    20, 54, 75
self-advocacy
  reflection on, 20
  skills, as learning, 10, 12, 21–22
social isolation, 2, 9, 29–30, 82, 120
stress
  avoid, as to escape from, 58,
    79–80, 92, 96
  coping with, 14–15, 53–54, 57, 67
  environment, as from,
    54, 56, 68
  physical reaction to, 3–4
success, tips for, 17–18, 21, 65

T

therapist
  finding, 12–14

trauma-focused, 11–12, 15
therapy
  behavioral, 10
  group, 11
  laughter as form of, 79
  professional, when
    necessary, 11, 65
trauma
  childhood, as in, 14
  growth after, 15
  mood, changes as normal, 76
  perception and, 93
  recovery from, 11, 87
  response to, as changing,
    60, 91–92
  symptoms of, 3, 9, 54,
    68, 80, 90
  treatment methods, 10
triggers
  identifying, 20, 61, 68
  response to, 60, 62, 66, 76, 93

V

violence
  characteristics of domestic,
    2–4, 31, 38, 48
  recovery from, 27, 69–70,
    102, 116
  treatment, methods of, 10,
    14–15, 120. *See also* resources

ABOUT THE AUTHOR

Stacie Freudenberg, PsyD, is a licensed clinical psychologist, speaker, and trauma expert. With over five years of experience specializing in domestic violence and sexual assault, Dr. Freudenberg has helped hundreds of survivors both during and following an abusive relationship. Additionally, she has provided domestic violence consultation for Child Protective Services throughout Colorado. Dr. Freudenberg is the owner of Luminate Psychological Services, a Colorado-based practice that offers trauma-informed therapy, consultation, and clinical supervision. On her days off, she enjoys biking through the mountains and spending time with her certified therapy dog, Theodore Tater Tott III.

CPSIA information can be obtained
at www.ICGtesting.com
Printed in the USA
JSHW011819100422
24755JS00003B/3